2023 UK Tower Vortx Digital Air Fryer Oven Cookbook

1500	Days Frugal, Tasty and Low calorie Air Fryer Recipes incl. Side Dishes, Desserts, Snacks and More

Maxine Land

CONTENTS

INTRODUCTION

A perfect recipe can only be prepared when all items are appropriately distributed. This means the quantity of every item is severely critical. But when you do not know how to cook, it becomes very hectic in the kitchen.

Because right now, you do not know anything. At that moment, a perfect recipe book can be a lifesaver. Tower Vortx Digital Air Fryer Oven Cookbook can be very useful for that. Here, you can get so many recipes for traditional food items, foreign cuisine, starters, breakfast, lunch, snacks, dinner, desserts, and much more.

This kitchen reference contains many important cuisines. This allows us to dive into those traditions. These recipes are going with the flow from generation to generation. Which means a lot of heart and soul goes into curating them.

CHAPTER 1 BASICS OF UK TOWER VORTX DIGITAL AIR FRYER OVEN

Understanding your Air Fryer

Now what is an air fryer and how does it work? So an air fryer is described as a small-scale countertop convection that deep fries food by using an insignificant amount of oil or just no oil. An air fryer's functioning is based on the famous Millard Reaction(you might have heard of it from burger tutorials online, where they keep repeating this name). The food here is in direct heat exposure and for a comparatively low amount of time while developing a crisp exterior and a tender interior.

The hot air that circulates from bottom to top is above 392°F (or 200° C). It is often said that ovens and air fryers are the same but it isn't 100% true because in an air fryer the air circulates in a guided passageway. Whereas in an oven the air is circulated from only one side and the rest is just idle air circulating.

Now, why would you want to buy and use an air fryer, like isn't your oven and your traditional stove enough? Yes, there's nothing wrong with your oven or your stove, it's just we are looking forward to saving some energy(both metaphorically and literally) and consuming better and healthier food.

So first of all, an air fryer takes half the amount of energy compared to an oven and it takes only 25 cents an hour to run. Plus it cuts down your monthly cost of buying oil because it just takes about a tablespoon of oil to cook a batch of food in an air fryer. And air fryers save a lot of time and hassle, starting from meal prep to cleaning utensils.

Plus you get a much healthier version of your favorite food. Like a healthier fired donut, a much less oily pizza, a healthier snack, or maybe a lighter tempura- your air fryer has got you covered. You know what you can even make desserts like chocolate cake, banana bread, a strawberry tart, and even gulab jamuns, now who knew that!

Airfryer is your new healthy bestie and yeah speaking of your bestie, you can try making try tasty air-fried food with your bestie, sounds like a plan right? And if you are a vegan, even better for you cause cooking vegan food in an air fryer just makes it 2x healthier. In short, just not owing an air fryer sounds like a huge loss to me, wouldn't you agree?

Start the Air Fryer Journey

Air Fryer is also eco-friendly because it uses a significantly less amount of electricity which means less carbon emission. And even though it seems like a very insignificant step but you are helping to reduce global warming and in reducing the mal effects of climate change.

Besides, using an air fryer means you are creating less waste. Plus you are not using oil much and thus there is less oil and grease produced hence, you are keeping the environment clean and healthy.

An air fryer keeps the heat trapped inside and avoids direct heat exposure outside its chamber so again less carbon emission. Now, if you're looking forward to contributing to reducing the effects of climate change this is a way to do it.

I guess I have talked a lot about the positive sides of air fryers and also have kind of persuaded you to buy one of them. Whether or not I was successful, I would like to tell you about the inspiration for my book.

I am a book author and just like every one of you guys, I don't get a lot of time for myself. In the free time I get I prefer spending it on something that I love. And for me it's cooking, I pour my heart and soul into it. But some days when it's just way too hectic and I am not into doing a lot of work or ordering junk food that's when an air fryer helped me.

It has become my literal kitchen bestie. I get to save some time, save my energy (and my money), and also it something a bit healthier. That sounds like a big win (or should I say multiple) for me.

I would love it if it makes others' lives much easier. So I tried, had my loved ones judge them, and finally wrote these recipes in a book for you. So yeah this book is very dear to me and I made this book into what it is just for you.

Thanks for managing to get so far, must have taken a lot of patience, and I appreciate that. I hope you will approve of these recipes as well and they will bring smiles to your face and your loved ones. My efforts and hopes will only be fulfilled if you try out these recipes and find this small attempt of mine helpful.

I thank those wholeheartedly who have stayed beside me in my journey and helped and guide me in making this book come to reality. It wouldn't have been possible without you.

Lots of love and best wishes to everyone. Cheers!

BASIC KITCHEN CONVERSIONS & EQUIVALENTS

DRY MEASUREMENTS CONVERSION CHART

3 TEASPOONS = 1 TABLESPOON = 1/16 CUP

6 TEASPOONS = 2 TABLESPOONS = 1/8 CUP

12 TEASPOONS = 4 TABLESPOONS = 1/4 CUP

24 TEASPOONS = 8 TABLESPOONS = 1/2 CUP

36 TEASPOONS = 12 TABLESPOONS = 3/4 CUP

48 TEASPOONS = 16 TABLESPOONS = 1 CUP

METRIC TO US COOKING CONVERSIONS

OVEN TEMPERATURES

120 °C = 250 °F

160 °C = 320 °F

180° C = 350 °F

205 °C = 400 °F

220 °C = 425 °F

LIQUID MEASUREMENTS CONVERSION CHART

8 FLUID OUNCES = 1 CUP = 1/2 PINT = 1/4 QUART

16 FLUID OUNCES = 2 CUPS = 1 PINT = 1/2 QUART

32 FLUID OUNCES = 4 CUPS = 2 PINTS = 1 QUART = 1/4 GALLON

128 FLUID OUNCES = 16 CUPS = 8 PINTS = 4 QUARTS = 1 GALLON

BAKING IN GRAMS

1 CUP FLOUR = 140 GRAMS

1 CUP SUGAR = 150 GRAMS

1 CUP POWDERED SUGAR = 160 GRAMS

1 CUP HEAVY CREAM = 235 GRAMS

VOLUME

1 MILLILITER = 1/5 TEASPOON

5 ML = 1 TEASPOON

15 ML = 1 TABLESPOON

240 ML = 1 CUP OR 8 FLUID OUNCES

1 LITER = 34 FL. OUNCES

WEIGHT

1 GRAM = .035 OUNCES

100 GRAMS = 3.5 OUNCES

500 GRAMS = 1.1 POUNDS

1 KILOGRAM = 35 OUNCES

US TO METRIC COOKING CONVERSIONS

1/5 TSP = 1 ML

1 TSP = 5 ML

1 TBSP = 15 ML

1 FL OUNCE = 30 ML

1 CUP = 237 ML

1 PINT (2 CUPS) = 473 ML

1 QUART (4 CUPS) = .95 LITER

1 GALLON (16 CUPS) = 3.8 LITERS

1 OZ = 28 GRAMS

1 POUND = 454 GRAMS

BUTTER

1 CUP BUTTER = 2 STICKS = 8 OUNCES = 230 GRAMS = 8 TABLESPOONS

WHAT DOES 1 CUP EQUAL

1 CUP = 8 FLUID OUNCES

1 CUP = 16 TABLESPOONS

1 CUP = 48 TEASPOONS

1 CUP = 1/2 PINT

1 CUP = 1/4 QUART

1 CUP = 1/16 GALLON

1 CUP = 240 ML

BAKING PAN CONVERSIONS

1 CUP ALL-PURPOSE FLOUR = 4.5 OZ

1 CUP ROLLED OATS = 3 OZ 1 LARGE EGG = 1.7 OZ

1 CUP BUTTER = 8 OZ 1 CUP MILK = 8 OZ

1 CUP HEAVY CREAM = 8.4 OZ

1 CUP GRANULATED SUGAR = 7.1 OZ

1 CUP PACKED BROWN SUGAR = 7.75 OZ

1 CUP VEGETABLE OIL = 7.7 OZ

1 CUP UNSIFTED POWDERED SUGAR = 4.4 OZ

BAKING PAN CONVERSIONS

9-INCH ROUND CAKE PAN = 12 CUPS

10-INCH TUBE PAN =16 CUPS

11-INCH BUNDT PAN = 12 CUPS

9-INCH SPRINGFORM PAN = 10 CUPS

9 X 5 INCH LOAF PAN = 8 CUPS

9-INCH SQUARE PAN = 8 CUPS

CHAPTER 2 BREAKFAST & SNACKS AND FRIES RECIPES

European Pancakes

Servings: 5

Ingredients:
- 3 large eggs
- 130g flour
- 140ml whole milk
- 2 tbsp unsweetened apple sauce
- A pinch of salt

Directions:
1. Set your fryer to 200°C and add five ramekins inside to heat up
2. Place all your ingredients inside a blender to combine
3. Spray the ramekins with a little cooking spray
4. Pour the batter into the ramekins carefully
5. Fry for between 6-8 minutes, depending on your preference
6. Serve with your favourite toppings

Cheesy Sausage Breakfast Pockets

Servings: 2

Ingredients:
- 1 packet of regular puff pastry
- 4 sausages, cooked and crumbled into pieces
- 5 eggs
- 50g cooked bacon
- 50g grated cheddar cheese

Directions:
1. Scramble your eggs in your usual way
2. Add the sausage and the bacon as you are cooking the eggs and combine well
3. Take your pastry sheets and cut rectangular shapes
4. Add a little of the egg and meat mixture to one half of each pastry piece
5. Fold the rectangles over and use a fork to seal down the edges
6. Place your pockets into your air fryer and cook at 190°C for 10 minutes
7. Allow to cool before serving

Bocconcini Balls

Servings: 2

Ingredients:
- 70 g/½ cup plus ½ tablespoon plain/all-purpose flour (gluten-free if you wish)
- 1 egg, beaten
- 70 g/1 cup dried breadcrumbs (gluten-free if you wish; see page 9)
- 10 bocconcini

Directions:
1. Preheat the air-fryer to 200°C/400°F.
2. Place the flour, egg and breadcrumbs on 3 separate plates. Dip each bocconcini ball first in the flour to coat, then the egg, shaking off any excess before rolling in the breadcrumbs.
3. Add the breaded bocconcini to the preheated air-fryer and air-fry for 5 minutes (no need to turn them during cooking). Serve immediately.

Tangy Breakfast Hash

Servings: 6

Ingredients:
- 2 tbsp olive oil
- 2 sweet potatoes, cut into cubes
- 1 tbsp smoked paprika
- 1 tsp salt
- 1 tsp black pepper
- 2 slices of bacon, cut into small pieces

Directions:
1. Preheat your air fryer to 200°C
2. Pour the olive oil into a large mixing bowl
3. Add the bacon, seasonings, potatoes and toss to evenly coat
4. Transfer the mixture into the air fryer and cook for 12-16 minutes
5. Stir after 10 minutes and continue to stir periodically for another 5 minutes

Delicious Breakfast Casserole

Servings: 4

Ingredients:
- 4 frozen hash browns
- 8 sausages, cut into pieces
- 4 eggs
- 1 diced yellow pepper
- 1 diced green pepper
- 1 diced red pepper
- Half a diced onion

Directions:
1. Line the bottom of your fryer with aluminium foil and arrange the hash browns inside
2. Add the sausage on top (uncooked)
3. Now add the onions and the peppers, sprinkling evenly
4. Cook the casserole on 170°C for around 10 minutes
5. Open your fryer and give the mixture a good stir
6. Combine the eggs in a small bowl and pour over the casserole, closing the lid
7. Cook for another 10 minutes on the same temperature
8. Serve with a little seasoning to taste

Muhammara

Servings: 4

Ingredients:
- 4 romano peppers
- 4 tablespoons olive oil
- 100 g/1 cup walnuts
- 90 g/1 heaped cup dried breadcrumbs (see page 9)
- 1 teaspoon cumin
- 2 tablespoons pomegranate molasses
- freshly squeezed juice of ½ a lemon
- ½ teaspoon chilli/chili salt (or salt and some chilli/hot red pepper flakes combined)
- fresh pomegranate seeds, to serve

Directions:
1. Preheat the air-fryer to 180°C/350°F.
2. Rub the peppers with ½ teaspoon of the olive oil. Add the peppers to the preheated air-fryer and air-fry for 8 minutes.
3. Meanwhile, lightly toast the walnuts by tossing them in a shallow pan over a medium heat for 3–5 minutes. Allow to cool, then grind the walnuts in a food processor. Once the peppers are cooked, chop off the tops and discard most of the seeds. Add to the food processor with all other ingredients. Process until smooth. Allow to cool in the fridge, then serve the dip with pomegranate seeds on top.

French Toast Slices

Servings: 1

Ingredients:
- 2 eggs
- 5 slices sandwich bread
- 100ml milk
- 2 tbsp flour
- 3 tbsp sugar
- 1 tsp ground cinnamon
- 1/2 tsp vanilla extract
- Pinch of salt

Directions:
1. Preheat your air fryer to 220°C
2. Take your bread and cut it into three pieces of the same size
3. Take a mixing bowl and combine the other ingredients until smooth
4. Dip the bread into the mixture, coating evenly
5. Take a piece of parchment paper and lay it inside the air fryer
6. Arrange the bread on the parchment paper in one layer
7. Cook for 5 minutes
8. Turn and cook for another 5 minutes

Blueberry Bread

Servings: 8

Ingredients:
- 260ml milk
- 3 eggs
- 25g protein powder
- 400g frozen blueberries
- 600g bisquick or pancake mixture

Directions:
1. Take a large mixing bowl and combine all ingredients until smooth
2. Preheat the air fryer to 250°C
3. Place the mixture into a loaf tin
4. Place the tin into the air fryer and cook for 30 minutes
5. A toothpick should come out clean if the bread is cooked

Toad In The Hole, Breakfast Style

Servings: 4

Ingredients:
- 1 sheet of puff pastry (defrosted)
- 4 eggs
- 4 tbsp grated cheese (cheddar works well)
- 4 slices of cooked ham, cut into pieces
- Chopped fresh herbs of your choice

Directions:
1. Preheat your air fryer to 200°C
2. Take your pastry sheet and place it on a flat surface, cutting it into four pieces
3. Take two of the pastry sheets and place them inside your fryer, cooking for up to 8 minutes, until done
4. Remove the pastry and flatten the centre down with a spoon, to form a deep hole
5. Add a tablespoon of the cheese and a tablespoon of the ham into the hole
6. Crack one egg into the hole
7. Return the pastry to the air fryer and cook for another 6 minutes, or until the egg is done as you like it
8. Remove and allow to cool
9. Repeat the process with the rest of the pastry remaining
10. Sprinkle fresh herbs on top and serve

Blanket Breakfast Eggs

Servings: 2

Ingredients:
- 2 eggs
- 2 slices of sandwich bread
- Olive oil spray
- Salt and pepper to taste

Directions:
1. Preheat your air fryer to 190°C and spray with a little oil
2. Meanwhile, take your bread and cut a hole into the middle of each piece
3. Place one slice inside your fryer and crack one egg into the middle
4. Season with a little salt and pepper
5. Cook for 5 minutes, before turning over and cooking for a further 2 minutes
6. Remove the first slice and repeat the process with the remaining slice of bread and egg

Mexican Breakfast Burritos

Servings: 6

Ingredients:
- 6 scrambled eggs
- 6 medium tortillas
- Half a minced red pepper
- 8 sausages, cut into cubes and browned
- 4 pieces of bacon, pre-cooked and cut into pieces
- 65g grated cheese of your choice
- A small amount of olive oil for cooking

Directions:
1. Into a regular mixing bowl, combine the eggs, bell pepper, bacon pieces, the cheese, and the browned sausage, giving everything a good stir
2. Take your first tortilla and place half a cup of the mixture into the middle, folding up the top and bottom and rolling closed
3. Repeat until all your tortillas have been used
4. Arrange the burritos into the bottom of your fryer and spray with a little oil
5. Cook the burritos at 170°C for 5 minutes

French Toast

Servings: 2

Ingredients:
- 2 beaten eggs
- 2 tbsp softened butter
- 4 slices of sandwich bread
- 1 tsp cinnamon
- 1 tsp nutmeg
- 1 tsp ground cloves
- 1 tsp maple syrup

Directions:
1. Preheat your fryer to 180°C
2. Take a bowl and add the eggs, salt, cinnamon, nutmeg, and cloves, combining well
3. Take your bread and butter each side, cutting into strips
4. Dip the bread slices into the egg mixture
5. Arrange each slice into the basket of your fryer
6. Cook for 2 minutes
7. Take the basket out and spray with a little cooking spray
8. Turn over the slices and place back into the fryer
9. Cook for 4 minutes
10. Remove and serve with maple syrup

Wholegrain Pitta Chips

Servings: 2

Ingredients:
- 2 round wholegrain pittas, chopped into quarters
- 1 teaspoon olive oil
- ½ teaspoon garlic salt

Directions:
1. Preheat the air-fryer to 180°C/350°F.
2. Spray or brush each pitta quarter with olive oil and sprinkle with garlic salt. Place in the preheated air-fryer and air-fry for 4 minutes, turning halfway through cooking. Serve immediately.

Easy Cheesy Scrambled Eggs

Servings: 1

Ingredients:
- 1 tbsp butter
- 2 eggs
- 100g grated cheese
- 2 tbsp milk
- Salt and pepper for seasoning

Directions:
1. Add the butter inside the air fryer pan and cook at 220°C until the butter has melted
2. Add the eggs and milk to a bowl and combine, seasoning to your liking
3. Pour the eggs into the butter panned cook for 3 minutes, stirring around lightly to scramble
4. Add the cheese and cook for another 2 more minutes

Swede Fries

Servings: 4

Ingredients:
- 1 medium swede/rutabaga
- ½ teaspoon salt
- ½ teaspoon freshly ground black pepper
- 1½ teaspoons dried thyme
- 1 tablespoon olive oil

Directions:
1. Preheat the air-fryer to 160°C/325°F.
2. Peel the swede/rutabaga and slice into fries about 6 x 1 cm/2½ x ½ in., then toss the fries in the salt, pepper, thyme and oil, making sure every fry is coated.
3. Tip into the preheated air-fryer in a single layer (you may need to cook them in two batches, depending on the size of your air-fryer) and air-fry for 15 minutes, shaking the drawer halfway through. Then increase the temperature to 180°C/350°F and cook for a further 5 minutes. Serve immediately.

Healthy Stuffed Peppers

Servings: 2

Ingredients:
- 1 large bell pepper, deseeded and cut into halves
- 1 tsp olive oil
- 4 large eggs
- Salt and pepper to taste

Directions:
1. Take your peppers and rub a little olive oil on the edges
2. Into each pepper, crack one egg and season with salt and pepper
3. You will need to insert a trivet into your air fryer to hold the peppers, and then arrange the peppers evenly
4. Set your fryer to 200°C and cook for 13 minutes
5. Once cooked, remove and serve with a little more seasoning, if required

Breakfast Eggs & Spinach

Servings: 4

Ingredients:
- 500g wilted, fresh spinach
- 200g sliced deli ham
- 1 tbsp olive oil
- 4 eggs
- 4 tsp milk
- Salt and pepper to taste
- 1 tbsp butter for cooking

Directions:
1. Preheat your air fryer to 180°C
2. You will need 4 small ramekin dishes, coated with a little butter
3. Arrange the wilted spinach, ham, 1 teaspoon of milk and 1 egg into each ramekin and season with a little salt and pepper
4. Place in the fryer 15 to 20 minutes, until the egg is cooked to your liking
5. Allow to cool before serving

Patatas Bravas

Servings: 4

Ingredients:
- 300g potatoes
- 1 tsp garlic powder
- 1 tbsp avocado oil
- 1 tbsp smoked paprika
- Salt and pepper to taste

Directions:
1. Peel the potatoes and cut them into cubes
2. Bring a large saucepan of water to the boil and add the potatoes, cooking for 6 minutes
3. Strain the potatoes and place them on a piece of kitchen towel, allowing to dry
4. Take a large mixing bowl and add the garlic powder, salt, and pepper and add the avocado oil, mixing together well
5. Add the potatoes to the bowl and coat liberally
6. Place the potatoes into the basket and arrange them with space in-between
7. Set your fryer to 200°C
8. Cook the potatoes for 15 minutes, giving them a shake at the halfway point
9. Remove and serve

Breakfast "pop Tarts"

Servings: 6

Ingredients:
- 2 slices of prepared pie crust, shortbread or filo will work fine
- 2 tbsp strawberry jam
- 60ml plain yogurt
- 1 tsp cornstarch
- 1 tsp Stevia sweetener
- 2 tbsp cream cheese
- A drizzle of olive oil

Directions:
1. Lay your pie crust flat and cut into 6 separate rectangular pieces
2. In a small bowl, mix together the cornstarch and the jam
3. Spread 1 tablespoon of the mixture on top of the crust
4. Fold each crust over to form the tart
5. Seal down the edges using a fork
6. Arrange your tarts inside the frying basket and spray with a little olive oil
7. Heat to 175°C and cook for 10 minutes
8. Meanwhile, combine the yogurt, cream cheese and Stevia in a bowl
9. Remove the tarts and allow to cool
10. Once cool, add the frosting on top and sprinkle with the sugar sprinkles

Whole Mini Peppers

Servings: 2

Ingredients:
- 9 whole mini (bell) peppers
- 1 teaspoon olive oil
- ¼ teaspoon salt

Directions:
1. Preheat the air-fryer to 180°C/350°F.
2. Place the peppers in a baking dish that fits in for your air-fryer and drizzle over the oil, then sprinkle over the salt.
3. Add the dish to the preheated air-fryer and air-fry for 10–12 minutes, depending on how 'chargrilled' you like your peppers.

Potato & Chorizo Frittata

Servings: 2

Ingredients:
- 3 eggs
- 1 sliced chorizo sausage
- 1 potato, boiled and cubed
- 50g feta cheese
- 50g frozen sweetcorn
- A pinch of salt
- 1 tbsp olive oil

Directions:
1. Add a little olive oil to the frying basket
2. Add the corn, potato, and sliced chorizo to the basket
3. Cook at 180°C until the sausage is a little brown
4. In a small bowl, beat together the eggs with a little seasoning
5. Pour the eggs into the pan
6. Crumble the feta on top
7. Cook for 5 minutes
8. Remove and serve in slices

Breakfast Doughnuts

Servings: 4

Ingredients:
- 1 packet of Pillsbury Grands
- 5 tbsp raspberry jam
- 1 tbsp melted butter
- 5 tbsp sugar

Directions:
1. Preheat your air fryer to 250°C
2. Place the Pillsbury Grands into the air fryer and cook for around 5m minutes
3. Remove and place to one side
4. Take a large bowl and add the sugar
5. Coat the doughnuts in the melted butter, coating evenly
6. Dip into the sugar and coat evenly once more
7. Using an icing bag, add the jam into the bag and pipe an even amount into each doughnut
8. Eat warm or cold

Easy Omelette

Servings: 1

Ingredients:
- 50ml milk
- 2 eggs
- 60g grated cheese, any you like
- Any garnishes you like, such as mushrooms, peppers, etc.

Directions:
1. Take a small mixing bowl and crack the eggs inside, whisking with the milk
2. Add the salt and garnishes and combine again
3. Grease a 6x3" pan and pour the mixture inside
4. Arrange the pan inside the air fryer basket
5. Cook at 170ºC for 10 minutes
6. At the halfway point, sprinkle the cheese on top
7. Loosen the edges with a spatula before serving

Oozing Baked Eggs

Servings: 2

Ingredients:
- 4 eggs
- 140g smoked gouda cheese, cut into small pieces
- Salt and pepper to taste

Directions:
1. You will need two ramekin dishes and spray each one before using
2. Crack two eggs into each ramekin dish
3. Add half of the Gouda cheese to each dish
4. Season and place into the air fryer
5. Cook at 350ºC for 15 minutes, until the eggs are cooked as you like them

Easy Air Fryer Sausage

Servings: 5

Ingredients:
- 5 uncooked sausages
- 1 tbsp mustard
- Salt and pepper for seasoning

Directions:
1. Line the basket of your fryer with parchment paper
2. Arrange the sausages inside the basket
3. Set to 180ºC and cook for 15 minutes
4. Turn the sausages over and cook for another 5 minutes
5. Remove and cool
6. Drizzle the mustard over the top and season to your liking

Healthy Breakfast Bagels

Servings: 2

Ingredients:
- 170g self raising flour
- 120ml plain yogurt
- 1 egg

Directions:
1. Take a large mixing bowl, combine the flour and the yogurt to create a dough
2. Cover a flat surface with a little extra flour and set the dough down
3. Create four separate and even balls
4. Roll each ball out into a rope shape and form a bagel with each
5. Take a small mixing bowl and whisk the egg
6. Brush the egg over the top of the bagel
7. Arrange the bagels inside your fryer evenly
8. Cook at 170ºC for 10 minutes
9. Allow to cool before serving

Cheese Scones

Servings:12 | **Ingredients:**

- ½ teaspoon baking powder
- 210 g/1½ cups self-raising/self-rising flour (gluten-free if you wish), plus extra for dusting
- 50 g/3½ tablespoons cold butter, cubed
- 125 g/1½ cups grated mature Cheddar
- a pinch of cayenne pepper
- a pinch of salt
- 100 ml/7 tablespoons milk, plus extra for brushing the tops of the scones

Directions:

1. Mix the baking powder with the flour in a bowl, then add the butter and rub into the flour to form a crumblike texture. Add the cheese, cayenne pepper and salt and stir. Then add the milk, a little at a time, and bring together into a ball of dough.
2. Dust your work surface with flour. Roll the dough flat until about 1.5 cm/⅝ in. thick. Cut out the scones using a 6-cm/2½-in. diameter cookie cutter. Gather the offcuts into a ball, re-roll and cut more scones – you should get about 12 scones from the mixture. Place the scones on an air-fryer liner or a piece of pierced parchment paper.
3. Preheat the air-fryer to 180°C/350°F.
4. Add the scones to the preheated air-fryer and air-fry for 8 minutes, turning them over halfway to cook the other side. Remove and allow to cool a little, then serve warm.

Crunchy Mexican Breakfast Wrap

Servings: 2

Ingredients:

- 2 large tortillas
- 2 corn tortillas
- 1 sliced jalapeño pepper
- 4 tbsp ranchero sauce
- 1 sliced avocado
- 25g cooked pinto beans

Directions:

1. Take each of your large tortillas and add the egg, jalapeño, sauce, the corn tortillas, the avocado and the pinto beans, in that order. If you want to add more sauce at this point, you can
2. Fold over your wrap to make sure that nothing escapes
3. Place each wrap into your fryer and cook at 190°C for 6 minutes
4. Remove your wraps and place in the oven, cooking for a further 5 minutes at 180°C, until crispy
5. Place each wrap into a frying pan and crisp a little more on a low heat, for a couple of minutes on each side

Plantain Fries

Servings: 2

Ingredients:
- 1 ripe plantain (yellow and brown outside skin)
- 1 teaspoon olive oil
- ¼ teaspoon salt

Directions:
1. Preheat the air-fryer to 180ºC/350ºF.
2. Peel the plantain and slice into fries about 6 x 1 cm/2½ x ½ in. Toss the fries in oil and salt, making sure every fry is coated.
3. Tip into the preheated air-fryer in a single layer (you may need to cook them in two batches, depending on the size of your air-fryer) and air-fry for 13–14 minutes until brown on the outside and soft on the inside. Serve immediately.

Courgette Fries

Servings: 2

Ingredients:
- 1 courgette/zucchini
- 3 tablespoons plain/all-purpose flour (gluten-free if you wish)
- ¼ teaspoon salt
- ¼ teaspoon freshly ground black pepper
- 60 g/¾ cup dried breadcrumbs (gluten-free if you wish; see page 9)
- 1 teaspoon dried oregano
- 20 g/¼ cup finely grated Parmesan
- 1 egg, beaten

Directions:
1. Preheat the air-fryer to 180ºC/350ºF.
2. Slice the courgette/zucchini into fries about 1.5 x 1.5 x 5 cm/⅝ x ⅝ x 2 in.
3. Season the flour with salt and pepper. Combine the breadcrumbs with the oregano and Parmesan.
4. Dip the courgettes/zucchini in the flour (shaking off any excess flour), then the egg, then the seasoned breadcrumbs.
5. Add the fries to the preheated air-fryer and air-fry for 15 minutes. They should be crispy on the outside but soft on the inside. Serve immediately.

CHAPTER 3 SAUCES & SNACK AND AP-PETISER RECIPES

Scotch Eggs

Servings: 6

Ingredients:
- 300g pork sausage
- 6 hard boiled eggs, shelled
- 50g cup flour
- 2 eggs, beaten
- 1 cup breadcrumbs
- Cooking spray

Directions:
1. Divide sausage into 6 portions
2. Place an egg in the middle of each portion and wrap around the egg
3. Dip the sausage in flour, then egg and then coat in breadcrumbs
4. Place in the air fryer and cook at 200ºC for 12 minutes

Thai Bites

Servings: 4

Ingredients:
- 400g pork mince
- 1 onion
- 1 tsp garlic paste
- 1 tbsp soy
- 1 tbsp Worcester sauce
- Salt and pepper
- 2 tsp Thai curry paste
- ½ lime juice and zest
- 1 tsp mixed spice
- 1 tsp Chinese spice
- 1 tsp coriander

Directions:
1. Place all ingredients in a bowl and mix well
2. Shape into balls
3. Place in the air fryer and cook at 180ºC for 15 minutes

Lumpia

Servings: 16

Ingredients:
- 400g Italian sausage
- 1 sliced onion
- 1 chopped carrot
- 50g chopped water chestnuts
- Cooking spray
- 2 cloves minced, garlic
- 2 tbsp soy sauce
- ½ tsp salt
- ¼ tsp ground ginger
- 16 spring roll wrappers

Directions:
1. Cook sausage in a pan for about 5 minutes. Add green onions, onions, water chestnuts and carrot cook for 7 minutes
2. Add garlic and cook for a further 2 minutes
3. Add the soy sauce, salt and ginger, stir to mix well
4. Add filling to each spring roll wrapper.
5. Roll over the bottom and tuck in the sides, continue to roll up the spring roll
6. Spray with cooking spray and place in the air fryer
7. Cook at 200ºC for 4 minutes turn and cook for a further 4 minutes

Mozzarella Sticks

Servings: 4

Ingredients:
- 60ml water
- 50g flour
- 5 tbsp cornstarch
- 1 tbsp cornmeal
- 1 tsp garlic powder
- ½ tsp salt
- 100g breadcrumbs
- ½ tsp pepper
- ½ tsp parsley
- ½ tsp onion powder
- ¼ tsp oregano
- ½ tsp basil
- 200g mozzarella cut into ½ inch strips

Directions:
1. Mix water, flour, cornstarch, cornmeal, garlic powder and salt in a bowl
2. Stir breadcrumbs, pepper, parsley, onion powder, oregano and basil together in another bowl
3. Dip the mozzarella sticks in the batter then coat in the breadcrumbs
4. Heat the air fryer to 200°C
5. Cook for 6 minutes turn and cook for another 6 minutes

Roasted Almonds

Servings: 2

Ingredients:
- 1 tbsp soy sauce
- 1 tbsp garlic powder
- 1 tsp paprika
- ¼ tsp pepper
- 400g raw almonds

Directions:
1. Place all of the ingredients apart from the almonds in a bowl and mix
2. Add the almonds and coat well
3. Place the almonds in the air fryer and cook at 160°C for 6 minutes shaking every 2 minutes

Mini Calzones

Servings: 16

Ingredients:
- Flour for rolling out the dough
- 1 round pizza dough
- 100g pizza sauce

Directions:
1. Roll out the dough to ¼ inch thick
2. Cut out 8-10 dough rounds using a cutter
3. Re-roll the dough and cut out another 6 rounds
4. Top each round with pizza sauce, cheese and pepperoni
5. Fold dough over and pinch the edges to seal
6. Heat the air fryer to 190°C
7. Place the calzone in the air fryer and cook for about 8 minutes until golden brown

Tortellini Bites

Servings: 6

Ingredients:
- 200g cheese tortellini
- 150g flour
- 100g panko bread crumbs
- 50g grated parmesan
- 1 tsp dried oregano
- 2 eggs
- ½ tsp garlic powder
- ½ tsp chilli flakes
- Salt
- Pepper

Directions:
1. Cook the tortellini according to the packet instructions
2. Mix the panko, parmesan, oregano, garlic powder, chilli flakes salt and pepper in a bowl
3. Beat the eggs in another bowl and place the flour in a third bowl
4. Coat the tortellini in flour, then egg and then in the panko mix
5. Place in the air fryer and cook at 185°C for 10 minutes until crispy
6. Serve with marinara sauce for dipping

Corn Nuts

Servings: 8

Ingredients:
- 1 giant white corn
- 3 tbsp vegetable oil
- 2 tsp salt

Directions:
1. Place the corn in a large bowl, cover with water and sit for 8 hours
2. Drain, pat dry and air dry for 20 minutes
3. Preheat the air fryer to 200ºC
4. Place in a bowl and coat with oil and salt
5. Cook in the air fryer for 10 minutes shake then cook for a further 10 minutes

Pork Jerky

Servings: 35

Ingredients:
- 300g mince pork
- 1 tbsp oil
- 1 tbsp sriracha
- 1 tbsp soy
- ½ tsp pink curing salt
- 1 tbsp rice vinegar
- ½ tsp salt
- ½ tsp pepper
- ½ tsp onion powder

Directions:
1. Mix all ingredients in a bowl until combined
2. Refrigerate for about 8 hours
3. Shape into sticks and place in the air fryer
4. Heat the air fryer to 160ºC
5. Cook for 1 hour turn then cook for another hour
6. Turn again and cook for another hour
7. Cover with paper and sit for 8 hours

Spring Rolls

Servings: 20

Ingredients:
- 160g dried rice noodles
- 1 tsp sesame oil
- 300g minced beef
- 200g frozen vegetables
- 1 onion, diced
- 3 cloves garlic, crushed
- 1 tsp soy sauce
- 1 tbsp vegetable oil
- 1 pack egg roll wrappers

Directions:
1. Soak the noodles in a bowl of water until soft
2. Add the minced beef, onion, garlic and vegetables to a pan and cook for 6 minutes
3. Remove from the heat, stir in the noodles and add the soy
4. Heat the air fryer to 175ºC
5. Add a diagonal strip of filling in each egg roll wrapper
6. Fold the top corner over the filling, fold in the two side corners
7. Brush the centre with water and roll to seal
8. Brush with vegetable oil, place in the air fryer and cook for about 8 minutes until browned

Focaccia Bread

Servings: 8

Ingredients:
- 500g pizza dough
- 3 tbsp olive oil
- 2-3 garlic cloves, chopped
- ¼ tsp red pepper flakes
- 50g parsley
- 1 tsp basil
- 100g chopped red peppers
- 60g black olives halved
- 60g green olives halved
- Salt and pepper to taste

Directions:
1. Preheat the air fryer to 180°C, make indentations in the pizza dough with your finger tips and set aside
2. Heat the olive oil in a pan add the garlic and cook for a few minutes, add the remaining ingredients and cook for another 5-8 minutes not letting the oil get too hot
3. Spread the oil mix over the dough with a spatula
4. Place in the air fryer and cook for 12-15 minutes

Jalapeño Pockets

Servings: 4

Ingredients:
- 1 chopped onion
- 60g cream cheese
- 1 jalapeño, chopped
- 8 wonton wrappers
- ¼ tsp garlic powder
- ⅛ tsp onion powder

Directions:
1. Cook the onion in a pan for 5 minutes until softened
2. Add to a bowl and mix with the remaining ingredients
3. Lay the wonton wrappers out and add filling to each one
4. Fold over to create a triangle and seal with water around the edges
5. Heat the air fryer to 200°C
6. Place in the air fryer and cook for about 4 minutes

Pao De Queijo

Servings: 20

Ingredients:
- 150g sweet starch
- 150g sour starch
- 50ml milk
- 25ml water
- 25ml olive oil
- 1 tsp salt
- 2 eggs
- 100g grated cheese
- 50g grated parmesan

Directions:
1. Preheat the air fryer to 170°C
2. Mix the starch together in a bowl until well mixed
3. Add olive oil, milk and water to a pan, bring to the boil and reduce the heat
4. Add the starch and mix until all the liquid is absorbed
5. Add the eggs and mix to a dough
6. Add the cheeses and mix well
7. Form the dough into balls
8. Line the air fryer with parchment paper
9. Bake in the air fryer for 8-10 minutes

Pasta Chips

Servings: 2

Ingredients:
- 300g dry pasta bows
- 1 tbsp olive oil
- 1 tbsp nutritional yeast
- 1½ tsp Italian seasoning
- ½ tsp salt

Directions:
1. Cook the pasta for half the time stated on the packet
2. Drain and mix with the oil, yeast, seasoning and salt
3. Place in the air fryer and cook at 200°C for 5 minutes shake and cook for a further 3 minutes until crunchy

Chicken & Bacon Parcels

Servings: 4

Ingredients:
- 2 chicken breasts, boneless and skinless
- 200ml BBQ sauce
- 7 slices of bacon, cut lengthwise into halves
- 2 tbsp brown sugar

Directions:
1. Preheat the air fryer to 220°C
2. Cut the chicken into strips, you should have 7 in total
3. Wrap two strips of the bacon around each piece of chicken
4. Brush the BBQ sauce over the top and sprinkle with the brown sugar
5. Place the chicken into the basket and cook for 5 minutes
6. Turn the chicken over and cook for another 5 minutes

Tostones

Servings: 4

Ingredients:
- 2 unripe plantains
- Olive oil cooking spray
- 300ml of water
- Salt to taste

Directions:
1. Preheat the air fryer to 200°C
2. Slice the tips off the plantain
3. Cut the plantain into 1 inch chunks
4. Place in the air fryer spray with oil and cook for 5 minutes
5. Remove the plantain from the air fryer and smash to ½ inch pieces
6. Soak in a bowl of salted water
7. Remove from the water and return to the air fryer season with salt cook for 5 minutes
8. Turn and cook for another 5 minutes

Popcorn Tofu

Servings: 4

Ingredients:
- 400g firm tofu
- 100g chickpea flour
- 100g oatmeal
- 2 tbsp yeast
- 150ml milk
- 400g breadcrumbs
- 1 tsp garlic powder
- 1 tsp onion powder
- 1 tbsp dijon mustard
- ½ tsp salt
- ½ tsp pepper
- 2 tbsp vegetable bouillon

Directions:
1. Rip the tofu into pieces. Place the breadcrumbs into a bowl, in another bowl mix the remaining ingredients
2. Dip the tofu into the batter mix and then dip into the breadcrumbs
3. Heat the air fryer to 175°C
4. Place the tofu in the air fryer and cook for 12 minutes shaking halfway through

Garlic Pizza Toast

Servings: 8

Ingredients:
- 1 pack garlic Texas toast, or 8 slices of bread topped with garlic butter
- 100g pizza sauce
- 50g pepperoni
- 100g grated cheese

Directions:
1. Top each piece of toast with pizza sauce
2. Add cheese and pepperoni
3. Heat air fryer to 190ºC
4. Place in the air fryer and cook for 5 minutes

Tasty Pumpkin Seeds

Servings: 2

Ingredients:
- 1 ¾ cups pumpkin seeds
- 2 tsp avocado oil
- 1 tsp paprika
- 1 tsp salt

Directions:
1. Preheat air fryer to 180ºC
2. Add all ingredients to a bowl and mix well
3. Place in the air fryer and cook for 35 minutes shaking frequently

Waffle Fries

Servings: 4

Ingredients:
- 2 large potatoes, russet potatoes work best
- 1 tsp salt for seasoning
- Waffle cutter

Directions:
1. Peel the potatoes and slice using the waffle cutter. You can also use a mandolin cutter that has a blade
2. Transfer the potatoes to a bowl and season with the salt, coating evenly
3. Add to the air fryer and cook at 220ºC for 15 minutes, shaking every so often

Korean Chicken Wings

Servings: 2

Ingredients:
- 25ml soy sauce
- 40g brown sugar
- 2 tbsp hot pepper paste
- 1 tsp sesame oil
- ½ tsp ginger paste
- ½ tsp garlic paste
- 2 green onions, chopped
- 400g chicken wings
- 1 tbsp vegetable oil

Directions:
1. Preheat air fryer to 200ºC
2. Place all ingredients apart from chicken wings and vegetable oil in a pan and simmer for about 4 minutes set aside
3. Massage the vegetable oil into the chicken wings
4. Place in the air fryer and cook for about 10 minutes
5. Turn and cook for a further 10 minutes
6. Coat the wings in the sauce and return to the air fryer
7. Cook for about 2 minutes

Italian Rice Balls

Servings: 2

Ingredients:
- 400g cooked rice
- 25g breadcrumbs, plus an extra 200g for breading
- 2 tbsp flour, plus an extra 2 tbsp for breading
- 1 tbsp cornstarch, plus an extra 3 tbsp for breading
- 1 chopped bell pepper
- 1 chopped onion
- 2 tbsp olive oil
- 1 tsp red chilli flakes
- 5 chopped mozzarella cheese sticks
- A little water for the breading
- Salt and pepper for seasoning

Directions:
1. Place the cooked rice into a bowl and mash with a fork. Place to one side
2. Take a saucepan and add the oil, salting the onion and peppers until they're both soft
3. Add the chilli flakes and a little salt and combine
4. Add the mixture to the mashed rice and combine
5. Add the 2 tbsp flour and 1 tbsp cornstarch, along with the 25g breadcrumbs and combine well
6. Use your hands to create balls with the mixture
7. Stuff a piece of the mozzarella inside the balls and form around it
8. Take a bowl and add the rest of the flour, corn starch and a little seasoning, with a small amount of water to create a thick batter
9. Take another bowl and add the rest of the breadcrumbs
10. Dip each rice ball into the batter and then the breadcrumbs
11. Preheat the air fryer to 220°C
12. Cook for 6 minutes, before shaking and cooking for another 6 minutes

Air-fried Pickles

Servings: 4

Ingredients:
- 1/2 cup mayonnaise
- 2 tsp sriracha sauce
- 1 jar dill pickle slices
- 1 egg
- 2 tbsp milk
- 50g flour
- 50g cornmeal
- ½ tsp seasoned salt
- ¼ tsp paprika
- ¼ tsp garlic powder
- ⅛ tsp pepper
- Cooking spray

Directions:
1. Mix the mayo and sriracha together in a bowl and set aside
2. Heat the air fryer to 200°C
3. Drain the pickles and pat dry
4. Mix egg and milk together, in another bowl mix all the remaining ingredients
5. Dip the pickles in the egg mix then in the flour mix
6. Spray the air fryer with cooking spray
7. Cook for about 4 minutes until crispy

Onion Bahji

Servings: 8

Ingredients:
- 1 sliced red onion
- 1 sliced onion
- 1 tsp salt
- 1 minced jalapeño pepper
- 150g chickpea flour
- 4 tbsp water
- 1 clove garlic, minced
- 1 tsp coriander
- 1 tsp chilli powder
- 1 tsp turmeric
- ½ tsp cumin

Directions:
1. Place all ingredients in a bowl and mix well, leave to rest for 10 minutes
2. Preheat air fryer to 175ºC
3. Spray air fryer with cooking spray.
4. Form mix into bahji shapes and add to air fryer
5. Cook for 6 minutes turn and cook for a further 6 minutes

Pepperoni Bread

Servings: 4

Ingredients:
- Cooking spray
- 400g pizza dough
- 200g pepperoni
- 1 tbsp dried oregano
- Ground pepper to taste
- Garlic salt to taste
- 1 tsp melted butter
- 1 tsp grated parmesan
- 50g grated mozzarella

Directions:
1. Line a baking tin with 2 inch sides with foil to fit in the air fryer
2. Spray with cooking spray
3. Preheat the air fryer to 200ºC
4. Roll the pizza dough into 1 inch balls and line the baking tin
5. Sprinkle with pepperoni, oregano, pepper and garlic salt
6. Brush with melted butter and sprinkle with parmesan
7. Place in the air fryer and cook for 15 minutes
8. Sprinkle with mozzarella and cook for another 2 minutes

Spicy Chickpeas

Servings: 4

Ingredients:
- 1 can chickpeas
- 1 tbsp yeast
- 1 tbsp olive oil
- 1 tsp paprika
- 1 tsp garlic powder
- ½ tsp salt
- Pinch cumin

Directions:
1. Preheat air fryer to 180ºC
2. Combine all ingredients
3. Add to the air fryer and cook for 22 minutes tossing every 4 minutes until cooked

Bacon Smokies

Servings: 8

Ingredients:
- 150g little smokies (pieces)
- 150g bacon
- 50g brown sugar
- Toothpicks

Directions:
1. Cut the bacon strips into thirds
2. Put the brown sugar into a bowl
3. Coat the bacon with the sugar
4. Wrap the bacon around the little smokies and secure with a toothpick
5. Heat the air fryer to 170ºC
6. Place in the air fryer and cook for 10 minutes until crispy

Mini Aubergine Parmesan Pizza

Servings: 8

Ingredients:
- 1 aubergine, cut into ½ inch slices
- Salt to taste
- 1 egg
- 1 tbsp water
- 100g bread crumbs
- 75g grated parmesan
- 6 tbsp pizza sauce
- 50g sliced olives
- 75g grated mozzarella
- Basil to garnish

Directions:
1. Preheat air fryer to 160ºC
2. Mix egg and water together and in another bowl mix the breadcrumbs and parmesan
3. Dip the aubergine in the egg then coat with the breadcrumbs
4. Place in the air fryer and cook for 10 minutes
5. Spoon pizza sauce on the aubergine, add olives and sprinkle with mozzarella
6. Cook for about 4 minutes until cheese has melted

Onion Pakoda

Servings: 2

Ingredients:
- 200g gram flour
- 2 onions, thinly sliced
- 1 tbsp crushed coriander seeds
- 1 tsp chilli powder
- ¾ tsp salt
- ¼ tsp turmeric
- ¼ tsp baking soda

Directions:
1. Mix all the ingredients together in a large bowl
2. Make bite sized pakodas
3. Heat the air fryer to 200°C
4. Line the air fryer with foil
5. Place the pakoda in the air fryer and cook for 5 minutes
6. Turn over and cook for a further 5 minutes

Snack Style Falafel

Servings: 15

Ingredients:
- 150g dry garbanzo beans
- 300g coriander
- 75g flat leaf parsley
- 1 red onion, quartered
- 1 clove garlic
- 2 tbsp chickpea flour
- Cooking spray
- 1 tbsp cumin
- 1 tbsp coriander
- 1 tbsp sriracha
- ½ tsp baking powder
- Salt and pepper to taste
- ¼ tsp baking soda

Directions:
1. Add all ingredients apart from the baking soda and baking powder to a food processor and blend well
2. Cover and rest for 1 hour
3. Heat air fryer to 190°C
4. Add baking powder and baking soda to mix and combine
5. Form mix into 15 equal balls
6. Spray air fryer with cooking spray
7. Add to air fryer and cook for 8-10 minutes

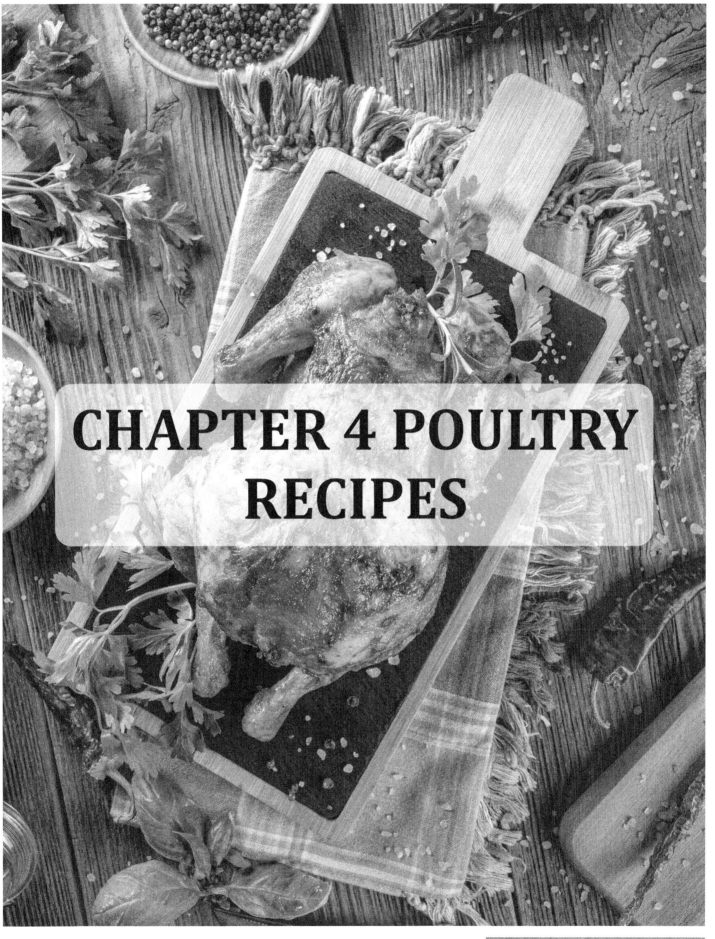

CHAPTER 4 POULTRY RECIPES

Crunchy Chicken Tenders

Servings: 4

Ingredients:
- 8 regular chicken tenders (frozen work best)
- 1 egg
- 2 tbsp olive oil
- 150g dried breadcrumbs

Directions:
1. Heat the fryer to 175ºC
2. In a small bowl, beat the egg
3. In another bowl, combine the oil and the breadcrumbs together
4. Take one tender and first dip it into the egg, and then cover it in the breadcrumb mixture
5. Place the tender into the fryer basket
6. Repeat with the rest of the tenders, arranging them carefully so they don't touch inside the basket
7. Cook for 12 minutes, checking that they are white in the centre before serving

Air Fryer Sesame Chicken Thighs

Servings: 4

Ingredients:
- 2 tbsp sesame oil
- 2 tbsp soy sauce
- 1 tbsp honey
- 1 tbsp sriracha sauce
- 1 tsp rice vinegar
- 400g chicken thighs
- 1 green onion, chopped
- 2 tbsp toasted sesame seeds

Directions:
1. Take a large bowl and combine the sesame oil, soy sauce, honey, sriracha and vinegar
2. Add the chicken and refrigerate for 30 minutes
3. Preheat the air fryer to 200ºC
4. Cook for 5 minutes
5. Flip and then cook for another 10 minutes
6. Serve with green onion and sesame seeds

Bacon Wrapped Chicken Thighs

Servings: 4

Ingredients:
- 75g softened butter
- ½ clove minced garlic
- ¼ tsp dried thyme
- ¼ tsp dried basil
- ⅛ tsp coarse salt
- 100g thick cut bacon
- 350g chicken thighs, boneless and skinless
- 2 tsp minced garlic
- Salt and pepper to taste

Directions:
1. Take a mixing bowl and add the softened butter, garlic, thyme, basil, salt and pepper, combining well
2. Place the butter onto a sheet of plastic wrap and roll up to make a butter log
3. Refrigerate for about 2 hours
4. Remove the plastic wrap
5. Place one bacon strip onto the butter and then place the chicken thighs on top of the bacon. Sprinkle with garlic
6. Place the cold butter into the middle of the chicken thigh and tuck one end of bacon into the chicken
7. Next, fold over the chicken thigh whilst rolling the bacon around
8. Repeat with the rest
9. Preheat the air fryer to 188C
10. Cook the chicken until white in the centre and the juices run clear

Chicken Parmesan With Marinara Sauce

Servings: 4

Ingredients:
- 400g chicken breasts, sliced in half
- 250g panko breadcrumbs
- 140g grated parmesan cheese
- 140g grated mozzarella cheese
- 3 egg whites
- 200g marinara sauce
- 2 tsp Italian seasoning
- Salt and pepper to taste
- Cooking spray

Directions:
1. Preheat the air fryer to 200°C
2. Lay the chicken slices on the work surface and pound with a mallet or a rolling pin to flatten
3. Take a mixing bowl and add the panko breadcrumbs, cheese and the seasoning, combining well
4. Add the egg whites into a separate bowl
5. Dip the chicken into the egg whites and then the breadcrumbs
6. Cook for 7 minutes in the air fryer

Keto Tandoori Chicken

Servings: 2

Ingredients:
- 500g chicken tenders, halved
- 1 tbsp minced ginger
- 1 tbsp minced garlic
- 1 tsp cayenne pepper
- 1 tsp turmeric
- 1 tsp garam masala
- 60ml yogurt
- 25g coriander leaves
- Salt and pepper to taste

Directions:
1. Take a large mixing bowl and combine all the ingredients, except the chicken
2. Once combined, add the chicken to the bowl and make sure it is fully coated
3. Preheat the air fryer to 160°C
4. Place the chicken in the air fryer and baste with oil
5. Cook for 10 minutes, turning over and then cooking for another 5 minutes
6. Serve whilst still warm

Satay Chicken Skewers

Servings: 4

Ingredients:
- 3 chicken breasts, chopped into 3 x 3-cm/1¼ x 1¼-in. cubes
- MARINADE
- 200 ml/¾ cup canned coconut milk (including the thick part from the can)
- 1 plump garlic clove, finely chopped
- 2 teaspoons freshly grated ginger
- 2 tablespoons soy sauce
- 1 heaped tablespoon peanut butter
- 1 tablespoon maple syrup
- 1 tablespoon mild curry powder
- 1 tablespoon fish sauce

Directions:
1. Mix the marinade ingredients thoroughly in a bowl, then toss in the chopped chicken and stir to coat thoroughly. Leave in the fridge to marinate for at least 4 hours.
2. Preheat the air-fryer to 190°C/375°F.
3. Thread the chicken onto 8 metal skewers. Add to the preheated air-fryer (you may need to cook these in two batches, depending on the size of your air-fryer). Air-fry for 10 minutes. Check the internal temperature of the chicken has reached at least 74°C/165°F using a meat thermometer – if not, cook for another few minutes and then serve.

Chicken Tikka Masala

Servings: 4

Ingredients:
- 100g tikka masala curry pasta
- 200g low fat yogurt
- 600g skinless chicken breasts
- 1 tbsp vegetable oil
- 1 onion, chopped
- 400g can of the whole, peeled tomatoes
- 20ml water
- 1 tbsp sugar
- 2 tbsp lemon juice
- 1 small bunch of chopped coriander leaves

Directions:
1. Take a bowl and combine the tikka masala curry paste with half the yogurt
2. Cut the chicken into strips
3. Preheat the air fryer to 200°C
4. Add the yogurt mixture and coat the chicken until fully covered
5. Place into the refrigerator for 2 hours
6. Place the oil and onion in the air fryer and cook for 10 minutes
7. Add the marinated chicken, tomatoes, water and the rest of the yogurt and combine
8. Add the sugar and lemon juice and combine again
9. Cook for 15 minutes

Sticky Chicken Tikka Drumsticks

Servings: 4

Ingredients:
- 12 chicken drumsticks
- MARINADE
- 100 g/½ cup Greek yogurt
- 2 tablespoons tikka paste
- 2 teaspoons ginger preserve
- freshly squeezed juice of ½ a lemon
- ¾ teaspoon salt

Directions:
1. Make slices across each of the drumsticks with a sharp knife. Mix the marinade ingredients together in a bowl, then add the drumsticks. Massage the marinade into the drumsticks, then leave to marinate in the fridge overnight or for at least 6 hours.
2. Preheat the air-fryer to 200°C/400°F.
3. Lay the drumsticks on an air-fryer liner or a piece of pierced parchment paper. Place the paper and drumsticks in the preheated air-fryer. Air-fry for 6 minutes, then turn over and cook for a further 6 minutes. Check the internal temperature of the drumsticks has reached at least 75°C/167°F using a meat thermometer – if not, cook for another few minutes and then serve.

Nashville Chicken

Servings: 4

Ingredients:
- 400g boneless chicken breast tenders
- 2 tsp salt
- 2 tsp coarsely ground black pepper
- 2 tbsp hot sauce
- 2 tbsp pickle juice
- 500g all purpose flour
- 3 large eggs
- 300ml buttermilk
- 2 tbsp olive oil
- 6 tbsp cayenne pepper
- 3 tbsp dark brown sugar
- 1 tsp chilli powder
- 1 tsp garlic powder
- 1 tsp paprika
- Salt and pepper to taste

Directions:
1. Take a large mixing bowl and add the chicken, hot sauce, pickle juice, salt and pepper and combine
2. Place in the refrigerator for 3 hours
3. Transfer the flour to a bowl
4. Take another bowl and add the eggs, buttermilk and 1 tbsp of the hot sauce, combining well
5. Press each piece of chicken into the flour and coat well
6. Place the chicken into the buttermilk mixture and then back into the flour
7. Allow to sit or 10 minutes
8. Preheat the air fryer to 193C
9. Whisk together the spices, brown sugar and olive oil to make the sauce and pour over the chicken tenders
10. Serve whilst still warm

Whole Chicken

Servings: 4

Ingredients:
- 1.5-kg/3¼-lb. chicken
- 2 tablespoons butter or coconut oil
- salt and freshly ground black pepper

Directions:
1. Place the chicken breast-side up and carefully insert the butter or oil between the skin and the flesh of each breast. Season.
2. Preheat the air-fryer to 180ºC/350ºF. If the chicken hits the heating element, remove the drawer to lower the chicken a level.
3. Add the chicken to the preheated air-fryer breast-side up. Air-fry for 30 minutes, then turn over and cook for a further 10 minutes. Check the internal temperature with a meat thermometer. If it is 75ºC/167ºF at the thickest part, remove the chicken from the air-fryer and leave to rest for 10 minutes before carving. If less than 75ºC/167ºF, continue to cook until this internal temperature is reached and then allow to rest.

Chicken & Potatoes

Servings: 4

Ingredients:
- 2 tbsp olive oil
- 2 potatoes, cut into 2" pieces
- 2 chicken breasts, cut into pieces of around 1" size
- 4 crushed garlic cloves
- 2 tsp smoked paprika
- 1 tsp thyme
- 1/2 tsp red chilli flakes
- Salt and pepper to taste

Directions:
1. Preheat your air fryer to 260ºC
2. Take a large bowl and combine the potatoes with half of the garlic, half the paprika, half the chilli flakes, salt, pepper and half the oil
3. Place into the air fryer and cook for 5 minutes, before turning over and cooking for another 5 minutes
4. Take a bowl and add the chicken with the rest of the seasonings and oil, until totally coated
5. Add the chicken to the potatoes mixture, moving the potatoes to the side
6. Cook for 10 minutes, turning the chicken halfway through

Chicken Balls, Greek-style

Servings: 4

Ingredients:
- 500g ground chicken
- 1 egg
- 1 tbsp dried oregano
- 1.5 tbsp garlic paste
- 1 tsp lemon zest
- 1 tsp dried onion powder
- Salt and pepper to taste

Directions:
1. Take a bowl and combine all ingredients well
2. Use your hands to create meatballs - you should be able to make 12 balls
3. Preheat your air fryer to 260°C
4. Add the meatballs to the fryer and cook for 9 minutes

Chicken Kiev

Servings: 4

Ingredients:
- 4 boneless chicken breasts
- 4 tablespoons plain/all-purpose flour (gluten-free if you wish)
- 1 egg, beaten
- 130 g/2 cups dried breadcrumbs (gluten-free if you wish, see page 9)
- GARLIC BUTTER
- 60 g/4 tablespoons salted butter, softened
- 1 large garlic clove, finely chopped

Directions:
1. Mash together the butter and garlic. Form into a sausage shape, then slice into 4 equal discs. Place in the freezer until frozen.
2. Make a deep horizontal slit across each chicken breast, taking care not to cut through to the other side. Stuff the cavity with a disc of frozen garlic butter. Place the flour in a shallow bowl, the egg in another and the breadcrumbs in a third. Coat each chicken breast first in flour, then egg, then breadcrumbs.
3. Preheat the air-fryer to 180°C/350°F.
4. Add the chicken Kievs to the preheated air-fryer and air-fry for 12 minutes until cooked through. This is hard to gauge as the butter inside the breast is not an indicator of doneness, so test the meat in the centre with a meat thermometer – it should be at least 75°C/167°F; if not, cook for another few minutes.

Air Fryer Chicken Thigh Schnitzel

Servings: 4

Ingredients:
- 300g boneless chicken thighs
- 160g seasoned breadcrumbs
- 1 tsp salt
- ½ tsp ground black pepper
- 30g flour
- 1 egg
- Cooking spray

Directions:
1. Lay the chicken on a sheet of parchment paper and add another on top
2. Use a mallet or a rolling pin to flatten it down
3. Take a bowl and add the breadcrumbs with the salt and pepper
4. Place the flour into another bowl
5. Dip the chicken into the flour, then the egg, and then the breadcrumbs
6. Preheat air fryer to 190°C
7. Place the chicken into the air fryer and spray with cooking oil
8. Cook for 6 minutes

Honey Cajun Chicken Thighs

Servings: 6

Ingredients:
- 100ml buttermilk
- 1 tsp hot sauce
- 400g skinless, boneless chicken thighs
- 150g all purpose flour
- 60g tapioca flour
- 2.5 tsp cajun seasoning
- ½ tsp garlic salt
- ½ tsp honey powder
- ¼ tsp ground paprika
- ⅛ tsp cayenne pepper
- 4 tsp honey

Directions:
1. Take a large bowl and combine the buttermilk and hot sauce
2. Transfer to a plastic bag and add the chicken thighs
3. Allow to marinate for 30 minutes
4. Take another bowl and add the flour, tapioca flour, cajun seasoning, garlic, salt, honey powder, paprika, and cayenne pepper, combining well
5. Dredge the chicken through the mixture
6. Preheat the air fryer to 175C
7. Cook for 15 minutes before flipping the thighs over and cooking for another 10 minutes
8. Drizzle 1 tsp of honey over each thigh

Thai Turkey Burgers

Servings: 4

Ingredients:
- 1 courgette/zucchini, about 200 g/7 oz.
- 400 g/14 oz. minced/ground turkey breast
- 35 g/½ cup fresh breadcrumbs (gluten-free if you wish)
- 1 teaspoon Thai 7 spice seasoning
- 1 teaspoon salt
- 1 teaspoon olive oil

Directions:
1. Coarsely grate the courgette/zucchini, then place in a piece of muslin/cheesecloth and squeeze out the water. Combine the grated courgette with all other ingredients except the olive oil, mixing together well. Divide the mixture into 4 equal portions and mould into burgers. Brush with oil.
2. Preheat the air-fryer to 190ºC/375ºC.
3. Add the turkey burgers to the preheated air-fryer and air-fry for 15 minutes, turning once halfway through cooking. Check the internal temperature of the burgers has reached at least 74ºC/165ºF using a meat thermometer – if not, cook for another few minutes and then serve.

Turkey And Mushroom Burgers

Servings: 2

Ingredients:
- 180g mushrooms
- 500g minced turkey
- 1 tbsp of your favourite chicken seasoning, e.g. Maggi
- 1 tsp onion powder
- 1 tsp garlic powder
- Salt and pepper to taste

Directions:
1. Place the mushrooms in a food processor and puree
2. Add all the seasonings and mix well
3. Remove from the food processor and transfer to a mixing bowl
4. Add the minced turkey and combine again
5. Shape the mix into 5 burger patties
6. Spray with cooking spray and place in the air fryer
7. Cook at 160ºC for 10 minutes, until cooked.

Orange Chicken

Servings: 2

Ingredients:
- 600g chicken thighs, boneless and skinless
- 2 tbsp cornstarch
- 60ml orange juice
- 1 tbsp soy sauce
- 2 tbsp brown sugar
- 1 tbsp rice wine vinegar
- 1/4 teaspoon ground ginger
- Pinch of red pepper flakes
- Zest of one orange
- 2 tsp water and 2 tsp cornstarch mixed together

Directions:
1. Preheat your air fryer to 250°C
2. Take a bowl and combine the chicken with the cornstarch
3. Place in the air fryer and cook for 9 minutes
4. Take a bowl and combine the rest of the ingredients, except for the water and cornstarch mixture
5. Place in a saucepan and bring to the boil and then turn down to a simmer for 5 minutes
6. Add the water and cornstarch mixture to the pan and combine well
7. Remove the chicken from the fryer and pour the sauce over the top

Chicken And Wheat Stir Fry

Servings: 4

Ingredients:
- 1 onion
- 1 clove of garlic
- 200g skinless boneless chicken breast halves
- 3 whole tomatoes
- 400ml water
- 1 chicken stock cube
- 1 tbsp curry powder
- 130g wheat berries
- 1 tbsp vegetable oil

Directions:
1. Thinly slice the onion and garlic
2. Chop the chicken and tomatoes into cubes
3. Take a large saucepan and add the water, chicken stock, curry powder and wheat berries, combining well
4. Pour the oil into the air fryer bowl and heat for 5 minutes at 200°C
5. Add the remaining ingredients and pour the contents into the air fryer
6. Cook for 15 minutes

Bbq Chicken Tenders

Servings: 6

Ingredients:
- 300g barbecue flavoured pork rinds
- 200g all purpose flour
- 1 tbsp barbecue seasoning
- 1 egg
- 400g chicken breast tenderloins
- Cooking spray

Directions:
1. Preheat the air fryer to 190°C
2. Place the pork rinds into a food processor and blitz to a breadcrumb consistency, before transferring to a bowl
3. In a separate bowl, combine the flour and barbecue seasoning
4. Beat the egg in a small bowl
5. Take the chicken and first dip into the egg, then the flour, and then the breadcrumbs
6. Place the chicken into the air fryer and spray with cooking spray and cook for about 15 minutes

Buffalo Chicken Wontons

Servings: 6

Ingredients:
- 200g shredded chicken
- 1 tbsp buffalo sauce
- 4 tbsp softened cream cheese
- 1 sliced spring onion
- 2 tbsp blue cheese crumbles
- 12 wonton wrappers

Directions:
1. Preheat the air fryer to 200ºC
2. Take a bowl and combine the chicken and buffalo sauce
3. In another bowl mix the cream cheese until a smooth consistency has formed and then combine the scallion blue cheese and seasoned chicken
4. Take the wonton wrappers and run wet fingers along each edge
5. Place 1 tbsp of the filling into the centre of the wonton and fold the corners together
6. Cook at 200ºC for 3 to 5 minutes, until golden brown

Smoky Chicken Breast

Servings: 2

Ingredients:
- 2 halved chicken breasts
- 2 tsp olive oil
- 1 tsp ground thyme
- 2 tsp paprika
- 1tsp cumin
- 0.5 tsp cayenne pepper
- 0.5 tsp onion powder
- Salt and pepper to taste

Directions:
1. In a medium bowl, combine the spices together
2. Pour the spice mixture onto a plate
3. Take each chicken breast and coat in the spices, pressing down to ensure an even distribution
4. Place the chicken to one side for 5 minutes
5. Preheat your air fryer to 180ºC
6. Arrange the chicken inside the fryer and cook for 10 minutes
7. Turn the chicken over and cook for another 10 minutes
8. Remove from the fryer and allow to sit for 5 minutes before serving

Turkey Cutlets In Mushroom Sauce

Servings: 2

Ingredients:
- 2 turkey cutlets
- 1 tbsp butter
- 1 can of cream of mushroom sauce
- 160ml milk
- Salt and pepper for seasoning

Directions:
1. Preheat the air fryer to 220ºC
2. Brush the turkey cults with the butter and seasoning
3. Place in the air fryer and cook for 11 minutes
4. Add the mushroom soup and milk to a pan and cook over the stone for around 10 minutes, stirring every so often
5. Top the turkey cutlets with the sauce

Chicken Fried Rice

Servings: 4

Ingredients:
- 400g cooked white rice
- 400g cooked chicken, diced
- 200g frozen peas and carrots
- 6 tbsp soy sauce
- 1 tbsp vegetable oil
- 1 diced onion

Directions:
1. Take a large bowl and add the rice, vegetable oil and soy sauce and combine well
2. Add the frozen peas, carrots, diced onion and the chicken and mix together well
3. Pour the mixture into a nonstick pan
4. Place the pan into the air fryer
5. Cook at 182C for 20 minutes

Chicken Milanese

Servings: 4

Ingredients:
- 130 g/1¾ cups dried breadcrumbs (gluten-free if you wish, see page 9)
- 50 g/⅔ cup grated Parmesan
- 1 teaspoon dried basil
- ½ teaspoon dried thyme
- ¼ teaspoon freshly ground black pepper
- 1 egg, beaten
- 4 tablespoons plain/all-purpose flour (gluten-free if you wish)
- 4 boneless chicken breasts

Directions:
1. Combine the breadcrumbs, cheese, herbs and pepper in a bowl. In a second bowl beat the egg, and in the third bowl have the plain/all-purpose flour. Dip each chicken breast first into the flour, then the egg, then the seasoned breadcrumbs.
2. Preheat the air-fryer to 180°C/350°F.
3. Add the breaded chicken breasts to the preheated air-fryer and air-fry for 12 minutes. Check the internal temperature of the chicken has reached at least 74°C/165°F using a meat thermometer – if not, cook for another few minutes.

Chicken Fajitas

Servings: 3

Ingredients:
- 2 boneless chicken breasts, sliced into strips
- 5 mini (bell) peppers, sliced into strips
- 1 courgette/zucchini, sliced into 5-mm/¼-in. thick discs
- 2 tablespoons olive oil
- 28-g/1-oz. packet fajita seasoning mix
- TO SERVE
- wraps
- sliced avocado
- chopped tomato and red onion
- grated Red Leicester cheese
- plain yogurt
- coriander/cilantro
- lime wedges, for squeezing

Directions:
1. Combine the chicken, (bell) peppers, courgettes/zucchini and olive oil in a bowl. Add the fajita seasoning and stir to coat.
2. Preheat the air-fryer to 180°C/350°F.
3. Add the coated vegetables and chicken to the preheated air-fryer and air-fry for 12 minutes, shaking the drawer a couple of times during cooking. Check the internal temperature of the chicken has reached at least 74°C/165°F using a meat thermometer – if not, cook for another few minutes.
4. Serve immediately alongside the serving suggestions or your own choices of accompaniments.

Grain-free Chicken Katsu

Servings: 4

Ingredients:

- 125 g/1¼ cups ground almonds
- ½ teaspoon salt
- ½ teaspoon garlic powder
- ½ teaspoon dried parsley
- ½ teaspoon freshly ground black pepper
- ¼ teaspoon onion powder
- ¼ teaspoon dried oregano
- 450 g/1 lb. mini chicken fillets
- 1 egg, beaten
- oil, for spraying/drizzling
- coriander/cilantro leaves, to serve
- KATSU SAUCE
- 1 teaspoon olive oil or avocado oil
- 1 courgette/zucchini (approx. 150 g/5 oz.), finely chopped
- 1 carrot (approx. 100 g/3½ oz.), finely chopped
- 1 onion (approx. 120 g/4½ oz.), finely chopped
- 1 eating apple (approx. 150 g/5 oz.), cored and finely chopped
- 1 teaspoon ground ginger
- 1 teaspoon ground turmeric
- 2 teaspoons ground cumin
- 2 teaspoons ground coriander
- 1½ teaspoons mild chilli/chili powder
- 1 teaspoon garlic powder
- 1½ tablespoons runny honey
- 1 tablespoon soy sauce (gluten-free if you wish)
- 700 ml/3 cups vegetable stock (700 ml/3 cups water with 1½ stock cubes)

Directions:

1. First make the sauce. The easiest way to ensure all the vegetables and apple are finely chopped is to combine them in a food processor. Heat the oil in a large saucepan and sauté the finely chopped vegetables and apple for 5 minutes. Add all the seasonings, honey, soy sauce and stock and stir well, then bring to a simmer and simmer for 30 minutes.

2. Meanwhile, mix together the ground almonds, seasonings and spices. Dip each chicken fillet into the beaten egg, then into the almond-spice mix, making sure each fillet is fully coated. Spray the coated chicken fillets with olive oil (or simply drizzle over).

3. Preheat the air-fryer to 180°C/350°F.

4. Place the chicken fillets in the preheated air-fryer and air-fry for 10 minutes, turning halfway through cooking. Check the internal temperature of the chicken has reached at least 74°C/165°F using a meat thermometer – if not, cook for another few minutes.

5. Blend the cooked sauce in a food processor until smooth. Serve the chicken with the Katsu Sauce drizzled over (if necessary, reheat the sauce gently before serving) and scattered with coriander leaves. Any unused sauce can be frozen.

Chicken And Cheese Chimichangas

Servings: 6

Ingredients:

- 100g shredded chicken (cooked)
- 150g nacho cheese
- 1 chopped jalapeño pepper
- 6 flour tortillas
- 5 tbsp salsa
- 60g refried beans
- 1 tsp cumin
- 0.5 tsp chill powder
- Salt and pepper to taste

Directions:

1. Take a large mixing bowl and add all of the ingredients, combining well

2. Add ⅓ of the filling to each tortilla and roll into a burrito shape

3. Spray the air fryer with cooking spray and heat to 200°C

4. Place the chimichangas in the air fryer and cook for 7 minutes

Pizza Chicken Nuggets

Servings: 2

Ingredients:
- 60 g/¾ cup dried breadcrumbs (see page 9)
- 20 g/¼ cup grated Parmesan
- ½ teaspoon dried oregano
- ¼ teaspoon freshly ground black pepper
- 150 g/⅔ cup Mediterranean sauce (see page 102) or 150 g/5½ oz. jarred tomato pasta sauce (keep any left-over sauce for serving)
- 400 g/14 oz. chicken fillets

Directions:
1. Preheat the air-fryer to 180°C/350°F.
2. Combine the breadcrumbs, Parmesan, oregano and pepper in a bowl. Have the Mediterranean or pasta sauce in a separate bowl.
3. Dip each chicken fillet in the tomato sauce first, then roll in the breadcrumb mix until coated fully.
4. Add the breaded fillets to the preheated air-fryer and air-fry for 10 minutes. Check the internal temperature of the chicken has reached at least 74°C/165°F using a meat thermometer – if not, cook for another few minutes.
5. Serve with some additional sauce that has been warmed through.

Chicken Tikka

Servings: 2

Ingredients:
- 2 chicken breasts, diced
- FIRST MARINADE
- freshly squeezed juice of ½ a lemon
- 1 tablespoon freshly grated ginger
- 1 tablespoon freshly grated garlic
- a good pinch of salt
- SECOND MARINADE
- 100 g/½ cup Greek yogurt
- ½ teaspoon chilli powder
- ½ teaspoon chilli paste
- ½ teaspoon turmeric
- ½ teaspoon garam masala
- 1 tablespoon olive oil

Directions:
1. Mix the ingredients for the first marinade together in a bowl, add in the chicken and stir to coat all the chicken pieces. Leave in the fridge to marinate for 20 minutes.
2. Combine the second marinade ingredients. Once the first marinade has had 20 minutes, add the second marinade to the chicken and stir well. Leave in the fridge for at least 4 hours.
3. Preheat the air-fryer to 180°C/350°F.
4. Thread the chicken pieces onto metal skewers that fit in your air-fryer. Add the skewers to the preheated air-fryer and air-fry for 10 minutes. Check the internal temperature of the chicken has reached at least 74°C/165°F using a meat thermometer – if not, cook for another few minutes and then serve.

CHAPTER 5 BEEF & LAMB AND PORK RECIPES

Meatballs In Tomato Sauce

Servings: 4

Ingredients:
- 1 small onion
- 300g minced pork
- 1 tbsp chopped parsley
- 1 tbsp thyme
- 1 egg
- 3 tbsp bread crumbs
- Salt and pepper to taste

Directions:
1. Place all ingredients into a bowl and mix well
2. Shape mixture into 12 meatballs
3. Heat the air fryer to 200ºC
4. Place the meatballs into the air fryer and cook for about 7 minutes
5. Tip the meatballs into an oven dish add the tomato sauce and cook for about 5 minutes in the air fryer until warmed through

Steak And Mushrooms

Servings: 4

Ingredients:
- 500g cubed sirloin steak
- 300g button mushrooms
- 3 tbsp Worcestershire sauce
- 1 tbsp olive oil
- 1 tsp parsley flakes
- 1 tsp paprika
- 1 tsp crushed chilli flakes

Directions:
1. Combine all ingredients in a bowl, cover and chill for at least 4 hours
2. Preheat air fryer to 200ºC
3. Drain and discard the marinade from the steak
4. Place the steak and mushrooms in the air fryer and cook for 5 minutes
5. Toss and cook for a further 5 minutes

Beef Satay

Servings: 2

Ingredients:
- 400g steak strips
- 2 tbsp oil
- 1 tbsp fish sauce
- 1 tsp sriracha sauce
- 200g sliced coriander (fresh)
- 1 tsp ground coriander
- 1 tbsp soy
- 1 tbsp minced ginger
- 1 tbsp minced garlic
- 1 tbsp sugar
- 25g roasted peanuts

Directions:
1. Add oil, dish sauce, soy, ginger, garlic, sugar sriracha, coriander and ¼ cup coriander to a bowl and mix. Add the steak and marinate for 30 minutes
2. Add the steak to the air fryer and cook at 200ºC for about 8 minutes
3. Place the steak on a plate and top with remaining coriander and chopped peanuts
4. Serve with peanut sauce

Beef Fried Rice

Servings: 2

Ingredients:
- 400g cooked rice
- 250g cooked beef strips
- 1 tbsp sesame oil
- 1 diced onion
- 1 egg
- 2 tsp garlic powder
- Salt and pepper
- 1 tbsp vegetable oil
- 250g frozen peas

Directions:
1. Preheat air fryer to 175°C
2. Season the beef with salt, pepper and garlic powder, cook in a pan until about ¾ cooked
3. Mix the rice with peas carrots and vegetable oil, add the beef and mix
4. Add to the air fryer and cook for about 10 minutes
5. Add the egg and cook until the egg is done

Salt And Pepper Belly Pork

Servings: 4

Ingredients:
- 500g belly pork
- 1 tsp pepper
- ½ tsp salt

Directions:
1. Cut the pork into bite size pieces and season with salt and pepper
2. Heat the air fryer to 200°C
3. Place in the air fryer and cook for 15 minutes until crisp

Vegetable & Beef Frittata

Servings: 2

Ingredients:
- 250g ground beef
- 4 shredded hash browns
- 8 eggs
- Half a diced onion
- 1 courgette, diced
- 250g grated cheese
- Salt and pepper for seasoning

Directions:
1. Break the ground beef up and place in the air fryer
2. Add the onion and combine well
3. Cook at 260°C for 3 minutes
4. Stir the mixture and cook foremother 2 minutes
5. Remove and clean the tray
6. Add the courgette to the air fryer and spray with a little cooking oil
7. Cook for 3 minutes
8. Add to the meat mixture and combine
9. Take a mixing bowl and combine the cheese, has browns, and eggs
10. Add the meat and courgette to the bowl and season with salt and pepper
11. Take a 6" round baking tray and add the mixture
12. Cook for 8 minutes before cutting lines in the top and cooking for another 8 minutes
13. Cut into slices before serving

Sausage Burritos

Servings:4 | Cooking Time:20 Minutes

Ingredients:
- 1 medium sweet potato
- 2 tbsp olive oil
- 1 tsp salt
- 1 tsp black pepper
- 8 sausages, uncooked
- 4 white flour tortillas
- 4 eggs, beaten
- 200 ml milk (any kind)
- 100 g / 3.5 oz cheddar cheese, grated

Directions:
1. Preheat the air fryer to 200 °C / 400 °F and line the air fryer mesh basket with parchment paper.
2. Peel the sweet potato and cut it into small chunks.
3. Place the sweet potato chunks in a bowl and toss in 1 tbsp olive oil. Sprinkle salt and pepper over the top.
4. Transfer the sweet potato chunks into the air fryer and cook for 8-10 minutes until hot. Remove from the air fryer and set aside to drain on paper towels.
5. Heat 1 tbsp olive oil in a medium frying pan and cook the sausages for 5-7 minutes until slightly browned. Remove the sausages and set them aside on paper towels to drain.
6. In a bowl, whisk together the beaten eggs and milk, and pour into the hot frying pan. Cook the eggs and use a fork to scramble them as they cook in the pan.
7. Once the eggs are cooked, mix them with the potatoes, sausages, and cheddar cheese in a bowl.
8. Spread the mixture evenly across the 4 white flour tortillas and roll them each up into tight burritos. Use a toothpick to keep them together if necessary.
9. Place the burritos into the hot air fryer and cook for 6-8 minutes, turning them over halfway through.
10. Enjoy the burritos for breakfast or lunch.

Tender Ham Steaks

Servings: 1

Ingredients:
- 1 ham steak
- 2 tbsp brown sugar
- 1 tsp honey
- 2 tbsp melted butter

Directions:
1. Preheat the air fryer to 220ºC
2. Combine the melted butter and brown sugar until smooth
3. Add the ham to the air fryer and brush both sides with the butter mixture
4. Cook for 12 minutes, turning halfway through and re-brushing the ham
5. Drizzle honey on top before serving

Lamb Burgers

Servings: 4

Ingredients:
- 600g minced lamb
- 2 tsp garlic puree
- 1 tsp harissa paste
- 2 tbsp Moroccan spice
- Salt and pepper

Directions:
1. Place all the ingredients in a bowl and mix well
2. Form into patties
3. Place in the air fryer and cook at 180ºC for 18 minutes

Southern Style Pork Chops

Servings: 4

Ingredients:
- 4 pork chops
- 3 tbsp buttermilk
- 100g flour
- Salt and pepper to taste
- Pork rub to taste

Directions:
1. Season the pork with pork rub
2. Drizzle with buttermilk
3. Coat in flour until fully covered
4. Place the pork chops in the air fryer, cook at 170ºC for 15 minutes
5. Turnover and cook for a further 10 minutes

Butter Steak & Asparagus

Servings: 6

Ingredients:
- 500g steak, cut into 6 pieces
- Salt and pepper
- 75g tamari sauce
- 2 cloves crushed garlic
- 400g asparagus
- 3 sliced peppers
- 25g balsamic vinegar
- 50g beef broth
- 2 tbsp butter

Directions:
1. Season steaks with salt and pepper
2. Place steaks in a bowl, add tamari sauce and garlic make sure steaks are covered, leave to marinate for at least 1hr
3. Place steaks on a board, fill with peppers and asparagus, roll the steak around and secure with tooth picks
4. Set your fryer to 200ºC and cook for 5 minutes.
5. Whilst cooking heat the broth, butter and balsamic vinegar in a saucepan until thickened
6. Pour over the steaks and serve

Kheema Meatloaf

Servings: 4

Ingredients:
- 500g minced beef
- 2 eggs
- 1 diced onion
- 200g sliced coriander
- 1 tbsp minced ginger
- $\frac{1}{8}$ cardamom pod
- 1 tbsp minced garlic
- 2 tsp garam masala
- 1 tsp salt
- 1 tsp cayenne
- 1 tsp turmeric
- $\frac{1}{2}$ tsp cinnamon

Directions:
1. Place all the ingredients in a large bowl and mix well
2. Place meat in an 8 inch pan and set air fryer to 180ºC
3. Place in the air fryer and cook for 15 minutes
4. Slice and serve

Pork Chilli Cheese Dogs

Servings: 2

Ingredients:
- 1 can of pork chilli, or chilli you have left over
- 200g grated cheese
- 2 hot dog bread rolls
- 2 hot dogs

Directions:
1. Preheat the air fryer to 260ºC
2. Cook the hot dogs for 4 minutes, turning halfway
3. Place the hotdogs inside the bread rolls and place back inside the air fryer
4. Top with half the cheese on top and then the chilli
5. Add the rest of the cheese
6. Cook for an extra 2 minutes

Beef Stirfry

Servings: 2

Ingredients:
- 500g steak
- 400g broccoli
- 3 peppers, cut into strips
- 1 tbsp ground ginger
- 25ml water
- 1 sliced onion
- 25g hoisin sauce
- 2 tsp minced garlic
- 1 tsp sesame oil
- 1 tbsp soy

Directions:
1. Add sesame oil, hoisin sauce, garlic, soy and water to a bowl and then add the steak, allow to marinate for 20 minutes
2. Mix 1 tbsp of oil with the vegetables and place in the air fryer, cook at 200ºC for about 5 minutes
3. Place the vegetables in a bowl and put aside
4. Add meat to air fryer and cook for 4 minutes, turn and cook for a further 2 minutes
5. Mix the steak with the vegetables and serve with rice

Sausage Gnocchi One Pot

Servings: 2

Ingredients:
- 4 links of sausage
- 250g green beans, washed and cut into halves
- 1 tsp Italian seasoning
- 1 tbsp olive oil
- 300g gnocchi
- Salt and pepper for seasoning

Directions:
1. Preheat the air fryer to 220ºC
2. Cut the sausage up into pieces
3. Take a bowl and add the gnocchi and green beans, along with the oil and season
4. Place the sausage into the fryer first and then the rest of the ingredients
5. Cook for 12 minutes, giving everything a stir halfway through

Pork Chops With Raspberry And Balsamic

Servings: 4

Ingredients:
- 2 large eggs
- 30ml milk
- 250g panko bread crumbs
- 250g finely chopped pecans
- 1 tbsp orange juice
- 4 pork chops
- 30ml balsamic vinegar
- 2 tbsp brown sugar
- 2 tbsp raspberry jam

Directions:
1. Preheat air fryer to 200°C
2. Mix the eggs and milk together in a bowl
3. In another bowl mix the breadcrumbs and pecans
4. Coat the pork chops in flour, egg and then coat in the breadcrumbs
5. Place in the air fryer and cook for 12 minutes until golden turning halfway
6. Put the remaining ingredients in a pan simmer for about 6 minutes, serve with the pork chops

German Rouladen

Servings: 2

Ingredients:
- 2 tbsp oil
- 2 cups sliced onion
- 4 tbsp sour cream
- 1 tbsp tomato paste
- 1 tsp chopped parsley
- 400g steak
- ¼ cup dijon mustard
- 4 bacon strips

Directions:
1. Add salt and pepper to the onions and mix
2. Cook the onions in the air fryer at 200°C for 5-6 minutes
3. Put half the onions in a bowl and mix with sour cream, 2 tsp parsley and tomato paste
4. Spread the mustard on to the steak then add the bacon and onion
5. Roll the steak up tightly and cook in the air fryer for 8-10 minutes

Copycat Burger

Servings: 4

Ingredients:
- 400g minced pork
- 4 wholemeal burger buns
- Avocado sauce to taste
- 1 avocado
- 1 small onion, chopped
- 2 chopped spring onions
- Salad garnish
- 1 tbsp Worcester sauce
- 1 tbsp tomato ketchup
- 1 tsp garlic puree
- 1 tsp mixed herbs

Directions:
1. In a bowl mix together the mince, onion, half the avocado and all of the seasoning
2. Form into burgers
3. Place in the air fryer and cook at 180°C for 8 minutes
4. When cooked place in the bun, layer with sauce and salad garnish

Cheesy Beef Enchiladas

Servings: 4

Ingredients:
- 500g minced beef
- 1 packet taco seasoning
- 8 tortillas
- 300g grated cheese
- 150g soured cream
- 1 can black beans
- 1 can chopped tomatoes
- 1 can mild chopped chillies
- 1 can red enchilada sauce
- 300g chopped coriander

Directions:
1. Brown the beef and add the taco seasoning
2. Add the beef, beans, tomatoes and chillies to the tortillas
3. Line the air fryer with foil and put the tortillas in
4. Pour the enchilada sauce over the top and sprinkle with cheese
5. Cook at 200ºC for five minutes, remove from air fryer add toppings and serve

Asian Meatballs

Servings: 2

Ingredients:
- 500g minced pork
- 2 eggs
- 100g breadcrumbs
- 1 tsp minced garlic
- ⅓ tsp chilli flakes
- 1 tsp minced ginger
- 1 tsp sesame oil
- 1 tsp soy
- 2 diced spring onions
- Salt and pepper to taste

Directions:
1. Mix all ingredients in a bowl until combined
2. Form mix into 1 ½ inch meatballs
3. Place in the air fryer and cook at 200ºC for about 10 minutes until cooked

Cheesy Meatball Sub

Servings: 2

Ingredients:
- 8 frozen pork meatballs
- 5 tbsp marinara sauce
- 160g grated parmesan cheese
- 2 sub rolls or hotdog rolls
- 1/4 tsp dried oregano

Directions:
1. Preheat the air fryer to 220ºC
2. Place the meatball in the air fryer and cook for around 10 minutes, turning halfway through
3. Place the marinara sauce in a bowl
4. Add the meatballs to the sauce and coat completely
5. Add the oregano on top and coat once more
6. Take the bread roll and add the mixture inside
7. Top with the cheese
8. Place the meatball sub back in the air fryer and cook for 2 minutes until the bad is toasted and the cheese has melted

Fillet Mignon Wrapped In Bacon

Servings: 2

Ingredients:
- 1 kg filet mignon
- 500g bacon slices
- Olive oil

Directions:
1. Wrap the fillets in bacon
2. Season with salt and pepper and brush with olive oil
3. Place in the air fryer cook at 200°C for 9 minutes turning halfway through

Steak Popcorn Bites

Servings: 4

Ingredients:
- 500g steak, cut into 1" sized cubes
- 500g potato chips, ridged ones work best
- 100g flour
- 2 beaten eggs
- Salt and pepper to taste

Directions:
1. Place the chips into the food processor and pulse unit you get fine chip crumbs
2. Take a bowl and combine the flour with salt and pepper
3. Add the chips to another bowl and the beaten egg to another bowl
4. Take the steak cubes and dip first in the flour, then the egg and then the chip crumbs
5. Preheat your air fryer to 260°C
6. Place the steak pieces into the fryer and cook for 9 minutes

Bbq Ribs

Servings: 2

Ingredients:
- 500g ribs
- 3 chopped garlic cloves
- 4 tbsp bbq sauce
- 1 tbsp honey
- ½ tsp five spice
- 1 tsp sesame oil
- 1 tsp salt
- 1 tsp black pepper
- 1 tsp soy sauce

Directions:
1. Chop the ribs into small pieces and place them in a bowl
2. Add all the ingredients into the bowl and mix well
3. Marinate for 4 hours
4. Preheat the air fryer to 180°C
5. Place the ribs into the air fryer and cook for 15 minutes
6. Coat the ribs in honey and cook for a further 15 minutes

Italian Meatballs

Servings: 12

Ingredients:
- 2 tbsp olive oil
- 2 tbsp minced shallot
- 3 cloves garlic minced
- 100g panko crumbs
- 35g chopped parsley
- 1 tbsp chopped rosemary
- 60ml milk
- 400g minced pork
- 250g turkey sausage
- 1 egg beaten
- 1 tbsp dijon mustard
- 1 tbsp finely chopped thyme

Directions:
1. Preheat air fryer to 200ºC
2. Heat oil in a pan and cook the garlic and shallot over a medium heat for 1-2 minutes
3. Mix the panko and milk in a bowl and allow to stand for 5 minutes
4. Add all the ingredients to the panko mix and combine well
5. Shape into 1 ½ inch meatballs and cook for 12 minutes

Cheese & Ham Sliders

Servings: 4

Ingredients:
- 8 slider bread rolls, cut in half
- 16 slices of sweet ham
- 16 slices of Swiss cheese
- 5 tbsp mayonnaise
- 1/2 tsp paprika
- 1 tsp onion powder
- 1 tsp dill

Directions:
1. Place 2 slices of ham into each bread roll and 2 slices of cheese
2. Take a bowl and combine the mayonnaise with the onion powder, dill and paprika
3. Add half a tablespoon of the sauce on top of each piece of cheese
4. Place the top on the bread slider
5. Cook at 220ºC for 5 minutes

Roast Pork

Servings: 4

Ingredients:
- 500g pork joint
- 1 tbsp olive oil
- 1 tsp salt

Directions:
1. Preheat air fryer to 180ºC
2. Score the pork skin with a knife
3. Drizzle the pork with oil and rub it into the skin, sprinkle with salt
4. Place in the air fryer and cook for about 50 minutes

Steak Fajitas

Servings: 4

Ingredients:
- 500g sliced steak
- 25g pineapple juice
- 2 tbsp lime juice
- 1 tbsp olive oil
- 1 tbsp soy sauce
- 1 tbsp minced garlic
- ½ tbsp chilli powder
- 1/2 tsp paprika
- 1 tsp cumin
- 1 pepper
- 1 onion
- Salt and pepper to taste

Directions:
1. Mix pineapple juice, lime juice, olive oil, soy sauce, garlic, cumin chilli powder and paprika. Pour over the steak and marinate for 4 hours
2. Line the air fryer with foil, add the peppers and onions, season with salt and pepper
3. Cook at 200ºC for 10 minutes, add the steak and cook for another 7 minutes
4. Serve with tortillas
5. Set your fryer to 170ºC and cook the sandwich for 4 minutes
6. Turn the sandwich over and cook for another 3 minutes
7. Turn the sandwich out and serve whilst hot
8. Repeat with the other remaining sandwich

Buttermilk Pork Chops

Servings: 4

Ingredients:
- 4 pork chops
- 3 tbsp buttermilk
- 75g flour
- Cooking oil spray
- 1 packet of pork rub
- Salt and pepper to taste

Directions:
1. Rub the chops with the pork rub
2. Place the pork chops in a bowl and drizzle with buttermilk
3. Coat the chops with flour
4. Place in the air fryer and cook at 190ºC for 15 minutes turning halfway

Beef Bulgogi Burgers

Servings: 4

Ingredients:
- 500g minced beef
- 2 tbsp gochujang
- 1 tbsp soy
- 2 tsp minced garlic
- 2 tsp minced ginger
- 2 tsp sugar
- 1 tbsp olive oil
- 1 chopped onion

Directions:
1. Mix all the ingredients in a large bowl, allow to rest for at least 30 minutes in the fridge
2. Divide the meat into four and form into patties
3. Place in the air fryer and cook at 180ºC for about 10 minutes
4. Serve in burger buns, if desired

CHAPTER 6 FISH & SEAFOOD RECIPES

Air Fried Scallops

Servings: 2

Ingredients:
- 6 scallops
- 1 tbsp olive oil
- Salt and pepper to taste

Directions:
1. Brush the filets with olive oil
2. Sprinkle with salt and pepper
3. Place in the air fryer and cook at 200ºC for 2 mins
4. Turn the scallops over and cook for another 2 minutes

Shrimp With Yum Yum Sauce

Servings: 4

Ingredients:
- 400g peeled jumbo shrimp
- 1 tbsp soy sauce
- 1 tbsp garlic paste
- 1 tbsp ginger paste
- 4 tbsp mayo
- 2 tbsp ketchup
- 1 tbsp sugar
- 1 tsp paprika
- 1 tsp garlic powder

Directions:
1. Mix soy sauce, garlic paste and ginger paste in a bowl. Add the shrimp, allow to marinate for 15 minutes
2. In another bowl mix ketchup, mayo, sugar, paprika and the garlic powder to make the yum yum sauce.
3. Set the air fryer to 200ºC, place shrimp in the basket and cook for 8-10 minutes

Air Fryer Mussels

Servings: 2

Ingredients:
- 400g mussels
- 1 tbsp butter
- 200ml water
- 1 tsp basil
- 2 tsp minced garlic
- 1 tsp chives
- 1 tsp parsley

Directions:
1. Preheat air fryer to 200ºC
2. Clean the mussels, soak for 30 minutes, and remove the beard
3. Add all ingredients to an air fryer-safe pan
4. Cook for 3 minutes
5. Check to see if the mussels have opened, if not cook for a further 2 minutes. Once all mussels are open, they are ready to eat.

Parmesan-coated Fish Fingers

Servings: 2

Ingredients:
- 350 g/12 oz. cod loins
- 1 tablespoon grated Parmesan
- 40 g/½ cup dried breadcrumbs (gluten-free if you wish, see page 9)
- 1 egg, beaten
- 2 tablespoons plain/all-purpose flour (gluten free if you wish)

Directions:
1. Slice the cod into 6 equal fish fingers/sticks.
2. Mix the Parmesan together with the breadcrumbs. Lay out three bowls: one with flour, one with beaten egg and the other with the Parmesan breadcrumbs. Dip each fish finger/stick first into the flour, then the egg and then the breadcrumbs until fully coated.
3. Preheat the air-fryer to 180°C/350°F.
4. Add the fish to the preheated air-fryer and air-fry for 6 minutes. Check the internal temperature of the fish has reached at least 75°C/167°F using a meat thermometer – if not, cook for another few minutes. Serve immediately.

Gluten Free Honey And Garlic Shrimp

Servings: 2

Ingredients:
- 500g fresh shrimp
- 5 tbsp honey
- 2 tbsp gluten free soy sauce
- 2 tbsp tomato ketchup
- 250g frozen stir fry vegetables
- 1 crushed garlic clove
- 1 tsp fresh ginger
- 2 tbsp cornstarch

Directions:
1. Simmer the honey, soy sauce, garlic, tomato ketchup and ginger in a saucepan
2. Add the cornstarch and whisk until sauce thickens
3. Coat the shrimp with the sauce
4. Line the air fryer with foil and add the shrimp and vegetables
5. Cook at 180°C for 10 minutes

Thai Salmon Patties

Servings: 7

Ingredients:
- 1 large can of salmon, drained and bones removed
- 30g panko breadcrumbs
- ¼ tsp salt
- 1 ½ tbsp Thai red curry paste
- 1 ½ tbsp brown sugar
- Zest of 1 lime
- 2 eggs
- Cooking spray

Directions:
1. Take a large bowl and combine all ingredients together until smooth
2. Use your hands to create patties that are around 1 inch in thickness
3. Preheat your air fryer to 180°C
4. Coat the patties with cooking spray
5. Cook for 4 minutes each side

Coconut Shrimp

Servings: 4

Ingredients:
- 250g flour
- 1 ½ tsp black pepper
- 2 eggs
- 150g unsweetened flaked coconut
- 1 Serrano chilli, thinly sliced
- 25g panko bread crumbs
- 300g shrimp raw
- ½ tsp salt
- 4 tbsp honey
- 25ml lime juice

Directions:
1. Mix together flour and pepper, in another bowl beat the eggs and in another bowl mix the panko and coconut
2. Dip each of the shrimp in the flour mix then the egg and then cover in the coconut mix
3. Coat the shrimp in cooking spray
4. Place in the air fryer and cook at 200ºC for 6-8 mins turning half way through
5. Mix together the honey, lime juice and chilli and serve with the shrimp

Thai Fish Cakes

Servings: 4

Ingredients:
- 200g pre-mashed potatoes
- 2 fillets of white fish, flaked and mashed
- 1 onion
- 1 tsp butter
- 1 tsp milk
- 1 lime zest and rind
- 3 tsp chilli
- 1 tsp Worcester sauce
- 1 tsp coriander
- 1 tsp mixed spice
- 1 tsp mixed herbs
- 50g breadcrumbs
- Salt and pepper to taste

Directions:
1. Cover the white fish in milk
2. in a mixing bowl place the fish and add the seasoning and mashed potatoes
3. Add the butter and remaining milk
4. Use your hands to create patties and place in the refrigerator for 3 hours
5. Preheat your air fryer to 200ºC
6. Cook for 15 minutes

Garlic Butter Salmon

Servings: 2

Ingredients:
- 2 salmon fillets, boneless with the skin left on
- 1 tsp minced garlic
- 2 tbsp melted butter
- 1 tsp chopped parsley
- Salt and pepper to taste

Directions:
1. Preheat the air fryer to 270 ºC
2. Take a bowl and combine the melted butter, parsley and garlic to create a sauce
3. Season the salmon to your liking
4. Brush the salmon with the garlic mixture, on both sides
5. Place the salmon into the fryer, with the skin side facing down
6. Cook for 10 minutes - the salmon is done when it flakes with ease

Crunchy Fish

Servings: 4

Ingredients:
- 200g dry breadcrumbs
- 4 tbsp olive oil
- 4 fillets of white fish
- 1 beaten egg
- 1 sliced lemon

Directions:
1. Heat the fryer to 180°C
2. In a medium mixing bowl, combine the olive oil and the breadcrumbs
3. Take the fish and first dip it into the egg and then the breadcrumbs, making sure they are evenly coated well
4. Arrange the fish into the basket
5. Cook for 12 minutes
6. Remove and serve with lemon slices

Peppery Lemon Shrimp

Servings: 2

Ingredients:
- 300g uncooked shrimp
- 1 tbsp olive oil
- 1 the juice of 1 lemon
- 0.25 tsp garlic powder
- 1 sliced lemon
- 1 tsp pepper
- 0.25 tsp paprika

Directions:
1. Heat the fryer to 200°C
2. Take a medium sized mixing bowl and combine the lemon juice, pepper, garlic powder, paprika and the olive oil together
3. Add the shrimp to the bowl and make sure they're well coated
4. Arrange the shrimp into the basket of the fryer
5. Cook for between 6-8 minutes, until firm and pink

Fish In Foil

Servings: 2

Ingredients:
- 1 tablespoon avocado oil or olive oil, plus extra for greasing
- 1 tablespoon soy sauce (or tamari)
- 1½ teaspoons freshly grated garlic
- 1½ teaspoons freshly grated ginger
- 1 small red chilli/chile, finely chopped
- 2 skinless, boneless white fish fillets (about 350 g/12 oz. total weight)

Directions:
1. Mix the oil, soy sauce, garlic, ginger and chilli/chile together. Brush a little oil onto two pieces of foil, then lay the fish in the centre of the foil. Spoon the topping mixture over the fish. Wrap the foil around the fish to make a parcel, with a gap above the fish but shallow enough to fit in your air-fryer basket.
2. Preheat the air-fryer to 180°C/350°F.
3. Add the foil parcels to the preheated air-fryer and air-fry for 7–10 minutes, depending on the thickness of your fillets. The fish should just flake when a fork is inserted. Serve immediately.

Oat & Parmesan Crusted Fish Fillets

Servings: 2

Ingredients:
- 20 g/⅓ cup fresh breadcrumbs
- 25 g/3 tablespoons oats
- 15 g/¼ cup grated Parmesan
- 1 egg
- 2 x 175-g/6-oz. white fish fillets, skin-on
- salt and freshly ground black pepper

Directions:
1. Preheat the air-fryer to 180°C/350°F.
2. Combine the breadcrumbs, oats and cheese in a bowl and stir in a pinch of salt and pepper. In another bowl beat the egg. Dip the fish fillets in the egg, then top with the oat mixture.
3. Add the fish fillets to the preheated air-fryer on an air-fryer liner or a piece of pierced parchment paper. Air-fry for 10 minutes. Check the fish is just flaking away when a fork is inserted, then serve immediately.

Cod In Parma Ham

Servings: 2

Ingredients:
- 2 x 175–190-g/6–7-oz. cod fillets, skin removed
- 6 slices Parma ham or prosciutto
- 16 cherry tomatoes
- 60 g/2 oz. rocket/arugula
- DRESSING
- 1 tablespoon olive oil
- 1½ teaspoons balsamic vinegar
- garlic salt, to taste
- freshly ground black pepper, to taste

Directions:
1. Preheat the air-fryer to 180°C/350°F.
2. Wrap each piece of cod snugly in 3 ham slices. Add the ham-wrapped cod fillets and the tomatoes to the preheated air-fryer and air-fry for 6 minutes, turning the cod halfway through cooking. Check the internal temperature of the fish has reached at least 60°C/140°F using a meat thermometer – if not, cook for another minute.
3. Meanwhile, make the dressing by combining all the ingredients in a jar and shaking well.
4. Serve the cod and tomatoes on a bed of rocket/arugula with the dressing poured over.

Store-cupboard Fishcakes

Servings: 3

Ingredients:
- 400 g/14 oz. cooked potato – either mashed potato or the insides of jacket potatoes (see page 124)
- 2 x 150–200-g/5½–7-oz. cans fish, such as tuna or salmon, drained
- 2 eggs
- ¾ teaspoon salt
- 1 teaspoon dried parsley
- ½ teaspoon freshly ground black pepper
- 1 tablespoon olive oil
- caper dressing (see page 79), to serve

Directions:
1. Mix the cooked potato, fish, eggs, salt, parsley and pepper together in a bowl, then divide into 6 equal portions and form into fishcakes. Drizzle the olive oil over both sides of each fishcake.
2. Preheat the air-fryer to 180°C/350°F.
3. Add the fishcakes to the preheated air-fryer and air-fry for 15 minutes, turning halfway through cooking. Serve with salad and tartare sauce or Caper Dressing.

Baked Panko Cod

Servings: 5

Ingredients:
- 400g cod, cut into 5 pieces
- 250g panko breadcrumbs
- 1 egg plus 1 egg white extra
- Cooking spray
- ½ tsp onion powder
- ½ tsp garlic salt
- ⅛ tsp black pepper
- ½ tsp mixed herbs

Directions:
1. Heat air fryer to 220°C
2. Beat the egg and egg white in a bowl
3. Sprinkle fish with herbs and spice mix, dip into the egg and then cover in the panko bread crumbs
4. Line air fryer basket with tin foil. Place the fish in the air fryer and coat with cooking spray
5. Cook for about 15 minutes until, fish is lightly browned

Garlic-parsley Prawns

Servings: 2

Ingredients:
- 300 g/10½ oz. raw king prawns/jumbo shrimp (without shell)
- 40 g/3 tablespoons garlic butter, softened (see page 72)
- 2 tablespoons freshly chopped flat-leaf parsley

Directions:
1. Thread the prawns/shrimp onto 6 metal skewers that will fit your air-fryer. Mix together the softened garlic butter and parsley and brush evenly onto the prawn skewers.
2. Preheat the air-fryer to 180°C/350°F.
3. Place the skewers on an air-fryer liner or a piece of pierced parchment paper. Add the skewers to the preheated air-fryer and air-fry for 2 minutes, then turn the skewers over and cook for a further 2 minutes. Check the internal temperature of the prawns has reached at least 50°C/120°F using a meat thermometer – if not, cook for another few minutes and serve.

Salt & Pepper Calamari

Servings: 2

Ingredients:
- 500g squid rings
- 500g panko breadcrumbs
- 250g plain flour
- 2 tbsp pepper
- 2 tbsp salt
- 200ml buttermilk
- 1 egg

Directions:
1. Take a medium bowl and combine the buttermilk and egg, stirring well
2. Take another bowl and combine the salt, pepper, flour, and panko breadcrumbs, combining again
3. Dip the quid into the buttermilk first and then the breadcrumbs, coating evenly
4. Place in the air fryer basket
5. Cook at 150°C for 12 minutes, until golden

Fish Taco Cauliflower Rice Bowls

Servings: 2

Ingredients:
- 400g fish of your choice, cut into strips
- 1 tsp chilli powder
- ½ tsp paprika
- 1 sliced avocado
- 25g pickled red onions
- 25g reduced fat sour cream
- ½ tsp cumin
- Salt and pepper to taste
- 300g cauliflower rice
- 1 tbsp lime juice
- 25g fresh coriander
- 1 tbsp sriracha

Directions:
1. Sprinkle both sides of the fish with chilli powder, cumin, paprika, salt and pepper
2. Heat the air fryer to 200°C, cook the fish for about 12 minutes
3. cook the cauliflower rice according to instructions, mix in lime juice and coriander once cooked
4. Divide the cauliflower rice between two bowls, add the sliced avocado, fish and pickled red onions.
5. Mix the sour cream with the sriracha and drizzle over the top

Mahi Fish Tacos

Servings: 4

Ingredients:
- 400g fresh mahi
- 8 small corn tortillas
- 2 tsp cajun seasoning
- 5 tbsp sour cream
- 2 tbsp mayonnaise
- 2 tbsp scotch bonnet pepper sauce (use 1 tbsp if you don't like your food too spicy)
- 1 tbsp sriracha sauce
- 2 tbsp lime juice
- Salt and pepper to taste
- 1 tbsp vegetable oil

Directions:
1. Clean the mahi. Cut into half inch slices and season with salt
2. Mix quarter parts cayenne pepper and black pepper with cajun seasoning. Sprinkle onto fish
3. Brush pepper sauce on both sides of the fish
4. Set the air fryer to 180°C and cook for about 10 minutes or until golden brown
5. Whilst the fish cooks make the chipotle lime cream. Mix the mayo, sour cream, lime juice sriracha and cayenne pepper
6. Assemble tacos and enjoy

Traditional Fish And Chips

Servings: 4

Ingredients:
- 4 potatoes, peeled and cut into chips
- 2 fish fillets of your choice
- 1 beaten egg
- 3 slices of wholemeal bread, grated into breadcrumbs
- 25g tortilla crisps
- 1 lemon rind and juice
- 1 tbsp parsley
- Salt and pepper to taste

Directions:
1. Preheat your air fryer to 200°C
2. Place the chips inside and cook until crispy
3. Cut the fish fillets into 4 slices and season with lemon juice
4. Place the breadcrumbs, lemon rind, parsley, tortillas and seasoning into a food processor and blitz to create a crumb consistency
5. Place the breadcrumbs on a large plate
6. Coat the fish in the egg and then the breadcrumb mixture
7. Cook for 15 minutes at 180°C

Tilapia Fillets

Servings: 2

Ingredients:
- 2 tbsp melted butter
- 150g almond flour
- 3 tbsp mayonnaise
- 2tilapia fillets
- 25g thinly sliced almonds
- Salt and pepper to taste
- Vegetable oil spray

Directions:
1. Mix the almond flour, butter, pepper and salt together in a bowl
2. Spread mayonnaise on both sides of the fish
3. Cover the fillets in the almond flour mix
4. Spread one side of the fish with the sliced almonds
5. Spray the air fryer with the vegetable spray
6. Place in the air fryer and cook at 160°C for 10 minutes

Shrimp Wrapped With Bacon

Servings: 2

Ingredients:
- 16 shrimp
- 16 slices of bacon
- 2 tbsp ranch dressing to serve

Directions:
1. Preheat the air fryer to 200°C
2. Wrap the shrimps in the bacon
3. Refrigerate for 30 minutes
4. Cook the shrimp for about 5 minutes turn them over and cook for a further 2 minutes
5. Serve with the ranch dressing on the side

Zesty Fish Fillets

Servings: 2

Ingredients:
- 30g dry ranch seasoning
- 2 beaten eggs
- 100g breadcrumbs
- 2.5 tbsp vegetable oil
- 4 fish fillets of your choice
- Wedges of lemon to serve

Directions:
1. Preheat the air fryer to 180°C
2. Mix the bread crumbs and seasoning together add the oil and combine
3. Dip the fish into the egg and then coat in the breadcrumb mix
4. Place in the air fryer and cook for 12 minutes
5. Serve with lemon wedges

Air Fryer Tuna

Servings: 2

Ingredients:
- 2 tuna steaks, boneless and skinless
- 2 tsp honey
- 1 tsp grated ginger
- 4 tbsp soy sauce
- 1 tsp sesame oil
- 1/2 tsp rice vinegar

Directions:
1. Combine the honey, soy sauce, rice vinegar and sesame oil in a bowl until totally mixed together
2. Cover the tuna steaks with the sauce and place in the refrigerator for half an hour to marinade
3. Preheat the air fryer to 270°C
4. Cook the tuna for 4 minutes
5. Allow to rest before slicing

Copycat Fish Fingers

Servings: 2

Ingredients:
- 2 slices wholemeal bread, grated into breadcrumbs
- 50g plain flour
- 1 beaten egg
- 1 white fish fillet
- The juice of 1 small lemon
- 1 tsp parsley
- 1 tsp thyme
- 1 tsp mixed herbs
- Salt and pepper to taste

Directions:
1. Preheat the air fryer to 180°C
2. Add salt pepper and parsley to the breadcrumbs and combine well
3. Place the egg in another bowl
4. Place the flour in a separate bowl
5. Place the fish into a food processor and add the lemon juice, salt, pepper thyme and mixed herbs
6. Blitz to create a crumb-like consistency
7. Roll your fish in the flour, then the egg and then the breadcrumbs
8. Cook at 180°C for 8 minutes

Fish In Parchment Paper

Servings: 2

Ingredients:
- 250g cod fillets
- 1 chopped carrot
- 1 chopped fennel
- 1 tbsp oil
- 1 thinly sliced red pepper
- ½ tsp tarragon
- 1 tbsp lemon juice
- 1 tbsp salt
- ½ tsp ground pepper

Directions:
1. In a bowl, mix the tarragon and ½ tsp salt add the vegetables and mix well
2. Cut two large squares of parchment paper
3. Spray the cod with oil and cover both sides with salt and pepper
4. Place the cod in the parchment paper and add the vegetables
5. Fold over the paper to hold the fish and vegetables
6. Place in the air fryer and cook at 170ºC for 15 minutes

Thai-style Tuna Fishcakes

Servings: 2

Ingredients:
- 200 g/7 oz. cooked potato
- 145 g/5 oz. canned tuna, drained
- 60 g/1 cup canned sweetcorn/corn kernels (drained weight)
- ½ teaspoon soy sauce
- ½ teaspoon fish sauce
- ½ teaspoon Thai 7 spice
- freshly squeezed juice of ½ a lime
- 1 teaspoon freshly grated garlic
- 1 teaspoon freshly grated ginger
- avocado or olive oil, for brushing
- LIME-ALMOND SATAY SAUCE
- 20 ml/4 teaspoons fresh lime juice
- 2 heaped tablespoons almond butter
- 1 teaspoon soy sauce
- ½ teaspoon freshly grated ginger
- ½ teaspoon freshly grated garlic
- ½ teaspoon avocado or olive oil
- ½ teaspoon maple syrup

Directions:
1. Combine all the fishcake ingredients in a food processor and blend together. Divide the mixture into 6 equal portions and mould into fishcakes. Brush a little oil over the top surface of the fishcakes.
2. Preheat the air-fryer to 180ºC/350ºF.
3. Place the fishcakes on an air-fryer liner or a piece of pierced parchment paper and add to the preheated air-fryer. Air-fry for 4 minutes, then turn over and brush the other side of each fishcake with oil and air-fry for a further 4 minutes.
4. To make the satay dipping sauce, mix all ingredients in a bowl with 1 tablespoon warm water. Serve alongside the fishcakes.

Pesto Salmon

Servings: 4

Ingredients:
- 4 x 150–175-g/5½–6-oz. salmon fillets
- lemon wedges, to serve
- PESTO
- 50 g/scant ½ cup toasted pine nuts
- 50 g/2 oz. fresh basil
- 50 g/⅔ cup grated Parmesan or Pecorino
- 100 ml/7 tablespoons olive oil

Directions:
1. To make the pesto, blitz the pine nuts, basil and Parmesan to a paste in a food processor. Pour in the olive oil and process again.
2. Preheat the air-fryer to 160ºC/325ºF.
3. Top each salmon fillet with 2 tablespoons of the pesto. Add the salmon fillets to the preheated air-fryer and air-fry for 9 minutes. Check the internal temperature of the fish has reached at least 63ºC/145ºF using a meat thermometer – if not, cook for another few minutes.

Ranch Style Fish Fillets

Servings: 4

Ingredients:
- 200g bread crumbs
- 30g ranch-style dressing mix
- 2 tbsp oil
- 2 beaten eggs
- 4 fish fillets of your choice
- Lemon wedges to garnish

Directions:
1. Preheat air fryer to 180ºC
2. Mix the bread crumbs and ranch dressing mix together, add in the oil until the mix becomes crumbly
3. Dip the fish into the, then cover in the breadcrumb mix
4. Place in the air fryer and cook for 12-13 minutes

CHAPTER 7 VEGE-
TARIAN & VEGAN
RECIPES

Courgette Meatballs

Servings: 4

Ingredients:
- 400g oats
- 40g feta, crumbled
- 1 beaten egg
- Salt and pepper
- 150g courgette
- 1 tsp lemon rind
- 6 basil leaves, thinly sliced
- 1 tsp dill
- 1 tsp oregano

Directions:
1. Preheat the air fryer to 200ºC
2. Grate the courgette into a bowl, squeeze any access water out
3. Add all the remaining ingredients apart from the oats and mix well
4. Blend the oats until they resemble breadcrumbs
5. Add the oats into the other mix and stir well
6. Form into balls and place in the air fryer cook for 10 minutes

Spanakopita Bites

Servings: 4

Ingredients:
- 300g baby spinach
- 2 tbsp water
- 100g cottage cheese
- 50g feta cheese
- 2 tbsp grated parmesan
- 1 tbsp olive oil
- 4 sheets of filo pastry
- 1 large egg white
- 1 tsp lemon zest
- 1 tsp oregano
- ¼ tsp salt
- ¼ tsp pepper
- ⅛ tsp cayenne

Directions:
1. Place spinach in water and cook for about 5 minutes, drain
2. Mix all ingredients together
3. Place a sheet of pastry down and brush with oil, place another on the top and do the same, continue until all four on top of each other
4. Ut the pastry into 8 strips then cut each strip in half across the middle
5. Add 1 tbsp of mix to each piece of pastry
6. Fold one corner over the mix to create a triangle, fold over the other corner to seal
7. Place in the air fryer and cook at 190ºC for about 12 minutes until golden brown

Spinach And Egg Air Fryer Breakfast Muffins

Servings:4 | Cooking Time:10 Minutes

Ingredients:
- 8 eggs
- 100 g / 3.5 oz fresh spinach
- 50 g / 1.8 oz cheddar cheese, grated
- ½ onion, finely sliced
- 1 tsp black pepper

Directions:
1. Preheat your air fryer to 200 °C / 400 °F and line an 8-pan muffin tray with parchment paper or grease with olive oil.
2. Gently press the spinach leaves into the bottom of each prepared muffin cup.
3. Sprinkle the finely sliced onion on top of the spinach.
4. Crack 2 eggs into each cup on top of the spinach and add some of the grated cheddar cheese on top of the eggs. Top with a light sprinkle of black pepper.
5. Carefully place the muffins into the air fryer basket and shut the lid. Bake for 10 minutes until the eggs are set and the muffins are hot throughout.
6. Serve the muffins while still hot for breakfast.

Ravioli Air Fryer Style

Servings: 4

Ingredients:
- Half a pack of frozen ravioli
- 200g Italian breadcrumbs
- 200ml buttermilk
- 5 tbsp marinara sauce
- 1 tbsp olive oil

Directions:
1. Preheat the air fryer to 220ºC
2. Place the buttermilk in a bowl
3. Add the breadcrumbs to another bowl
4. Take each piece of ravioli and dip it first into the buttermilk and then into the breadcrumbs, coating evenly
5. Add the ravioli to the air fryer and cook for 7 minutes, adding a small amount of oil at the halfway point
6. Serve with the marinara sauce on the side

Cheese, Tomato & Pesto Crustless Quiches

Servings: 1–2

Ingredients:
- 40 g/½ cup grated mature Cheddar
- 3 eggs, beaten
- 3 cherry tomatoes, finely chopped
- salt and freshly ground black pepper
- ½ teaspoon olive oil, to grease ramekins
- 2 tablespoons pesto (jarred or see page 80)

Directions:
1. Preheat the air-fryer to 180ºC/350ºF.
2. Mix together the cheese, eggs, tomatoes, salt and pepper in a bowl.
3. Grease the ramekins with the oil (and line with parchment paper if you wish to remove the quiches to serve). Pour the egg mixture into the ramekins.
4. Place the ramekins in the preheated air-fryer and air-fry for 10 minutes, stirring the contents of the ramekins halfway through cooking. Serve hot with 1 tablespoon pesto drizzled over each quiche.

Jackfruit Taquitos

Servings: 2

Ingredients:
- 1 large Jackfruit
- 250g red beans
- 100g pico de gallo sauce
- 50ml water
- 2 tbsp water
- 4 wheat tortillas
- Olive oil spray

Directions:
1. Place the jackfruit, red beans, sauce and water in a saucepan
2. Bring to the boil and simmer for 25 minutes
3. Preheat the air fryer to 185ºC
4. Mash the jackfruit mixture, add ¼ cup of the mix to each tortilla and roll up tightly
5. Spray with olive oil and place in the air fryer
6. Cook for 8 minutes

Quinoa-stuffed Romano Peppers

Servings: 2

Ingredients:
- 1 tablespoon olive oil
- 1 onion, diced
- 1 garlic clove, chopped
- 100 g/⅔ cup uncooked quinoa
- 1½ tablespoons fajita seasoning
- 140 g/1 cup canned sweetcorn/corn kernels (drained weight)
- 3 romano peppers, sliced lengthways, seeds removed but stalk left intact
- 60 g/⅔ cup grated mature Cheddar

Directions:
1. Heat the oil in a saucepan. Add the onion and garlic and sauté for 5 minutes, until soft. Add the quinoa, fajita seasoning and 250 ml/1 cup water. Bring to a simmer, then cover with a lid and simmer for 15 minutes or until the quinoa is cooked and the water absorbed. Stir in the sweetcorn/corn kernels. Stuff each pepper half with the quinoa mixture, then top with grated cheese.
2. Preheat the air-fryer to 180ºC/350ºF.
3. Place the peppers on an air-fryer liner or a piece of pierced parchment paper, place in the preheated air-fryer and air-fry for 12–14 minutes, depending how 'chargrilled' you like your peppers.

Sweet Potato Taquitos

Servings: 10

Ingredients:
- 1 sweet potato cut into ½ inch pieces
- 1 ½ tsp oil
- 1 chopped onion
- 1 tsp minced garlic
- 400g black beans
- 3 tbsp water
- 10 corn tortillas
- 1 chipotle pepper, chopped
- ½ tsp cumin
- ½ tsp paprika
- ½ chilli powder
- ⅛ tsp salt
- ½ tsp maple syrup

Directions:
1. Place the sweet potato in the air fryer spray with oil and cook for 12 minutes at 200ºC
2. Heat oil in a pan, add the onion and garlic and cook for a few minutes until soft
3. Add remaining ingredients to the pan, add 2 tbsp of water and combine
4. Add the sweet potato and 1 tbsp of water and mix
5. Warm the tortilla in the microwave for about 1 minute
6. Place a row of filling across the centre of each tortilla. Fold up the bottom of the tortilla, tuck under the filling, fold in the edges then continue to roll the tortilla
7. Place in the air fryer and cook for about 12 minutes

Orange Zingy Cauliflower

Servings: 2

Ingredients:
- 200ml water
- 200g flour
- Half the head of a cauliflower, cut into 1.5" florets
- 2 tsp olive oil
- 2 minced garlic cloves
- 1 tsp minced ginger
- 150ml orange juice
- 3 tbsp white vinegar
- 1/2 tsp red pepper flakes
- 1 tsp sesame oil 100g brown sugar
- 3 tbsp soy sauce
- 1 tbsp cornstarch
- 2 tbsp water
- 1 tsp salt

Directions:
1. Take a medium mixing bowl and add the water, salt and flour together
2. Dip each floret of cauliflower into the mixture and place in the air fryer basket
3. Cook at 220°C for 15 minutes
4. Meanwhile make the orange sauce by combining all ingredients in a saucepan and allowing to simmer for 3 minutes, until the sauce has thickened
5. Drizzle the sauce over the cauliflower to serve

Aubergine Dip

Servings: 4

Ingredients:
- 1 aubergine
- 2 tsp oil
- 3 tbsp tahini
- 1 tbsp lemon juice
- 1 clove garlic minced
- 1/8 tsp cumin
- 1/4 tsp smoked salt
- 1/8 tsp salt
- Drizzle olive oil

Directions:
1. Cut the aubergine in half length wise and coat in oil, Place in the air fryer and cook at 200°C for 20 minutes
2. Remove from the air fryer and allow to cool
3. Scoop out the aubergine from the peel and put in a food processor
4. Add all the remaining ingredients, blend to combine but not to a puree
5. Serve with a drizzle of olive oil

Bagel Pizza

Servings: 1

Ingredients:
- 1 bagel
- 2 tbsp marinara sauce
- 6 slices vegan pepperoni
- 2 tbsp mozzarella
- Pinch of basil

Directions:
1. Heat the air fryer to 180°C
2. Cut the bagel in half and toast for 2 minutes in the air fryer
3. Remove from the air fryer and top with marinara sauce, pepperoni and mozzarella
4. Return to the air fryer and cook for 4-5 minutes
5. Sprinkle with basil to serve

Chickpea And Sweetcorn Falafel

Servings:4 | Cooking Time:15 Minutes

Ingredients:
- ½ onion, sliced
- 2 cloves garlic, peeled and sliced
- 2 tbsp fresh parsley, chopped
- 2 tbsp fresh coriander, chopped
- 2 x 400 g / 14 oz chickpeas, drained and rinsed
- 1 tsp salt
- 1 tsp black pepper
- 1 tsp baking powder
- 1 tsp dried mixed herbs
- 1 tsp cumin
- 1 tsp chili powder
- 50 g / 1.8 oz sweetcorn, fresh or frozen

Directions:
1. Preheat the air fryer to 180 °C / 350 °F and line the bottom of the basket with parchment paper.
2. In a food processor, place the onion, garlic cloves, fresh parsley, and fresh coriander. Pulse the ingredients in 30-second intervals until they form a smooth mixture. Scrape the mixture from the sides of the food processor in between each interval if necessary.
3. Mix in the chickpeas, salt, black pepper, baking powder, dried mixed herbs, cumin, and chili powder. Pulse the mixture until fully combined and smooth. Add more water if the mixture is looking a bit dry. The mixture should be dry but not crumbly.
4. Use a spoon to scoop out 2 tbsp of the chickpea mixture at a time and roll into small, even falafels.
5. Transfer the falafels into the prepared air fryer basket and cook for 12-15 minutes.
6. Serve the falafels either hot or cold as a side dish to your main meal or as part of a large salad.

Roast Vegetables

Servings: 4

Ingredients:
- 100g diced courgette
- 100g diced squash
- 100g diced mushrooms
- 100g diced cauliflower
- 100g diced asparagus
- 100g diced pepper
- 2 tsp oil
- ½ tsp salt
- ¼ tsp pepper
- ¼ tsp seasoning

Directions:
1. Preheat air fryer to 180ºC
2. Mix all ingredients together
3. Add to air fryer and cook for 10 minutes stirring halfway

Roast Cauliflower & Broccoli

Servings: 6

Ingredients:
- 300g broccoli
- 300g cauliflower
- 2 tbsp oil
- ½ tsp garlic powder
- ¼ tsp salt
- ¼ tsp paprika
- ⅛ tsp pepper

Directions:
1. Preheat air fryer to 200ºC
2. Place broccoli and cauliflower in a bowl and microwave for 3 minutes
3. Add remaining ingredients and mix well
4. Add to the air fryer and cook for about 12 mins

Tomato And Herb Tofu

Servings:4 | Cooking Time:10 Minutes

Ingredients:
- 1 x 400 g / 14 oz block firm tofu
- 1 tbsp soy sauce
- 2 tbsp tomato paste
- 1 tsp dried oregano
- 1 tsp dried basil
- 1 tsp garlic powder

Directions:
1. Remove the tofu from the packaging and place on a sheet of kitchen roll. Place another sheet of kitchen roll on top of the tofu and place a plate on top of it.
2. Use something heavy to press the plate down on top of the tofu. Leave for 10 minutes to press the water out of the tofu.
3. Remove the paper towels from the tofu and chop them into even slices that are around ½ cm thick.
4. Preheat the air fryer to 180 °C / 350 °F. Remove the mesh basket from the air fryer machine and line with parchment paper.
5. Place the tofu slices on a lined baking sheet.
6. In a bowl, mix the soy sauce, tomato paste, dried oregano, dried basil, and garlic powder until fully combined.
7. Spread the mixture evenly over the tofu slices. Place the tofu slices on the baking sheet in the lined air fryer basket and cook for 10 minutes until the tofu is firm and crispy.
8. Serve the tofu slices with a side of rice or noodles and some hot vegetables.

Flat Mushroom Pizzas

Servings: 1

Ingredients:
- 2 portobello mushrooms, cleaned and stalk removed
- 6 mozzarella balls
- 1 teaspoon olive oil
- PIZZA SAUCE
- 100 g/3½ oz. passata/strained tomatoes
- 1 teaspoon dried oregano
- ¼ teaspoon garlic salt

Directions:
1. Preheat the air-fryer to 180ºC/350ºF.
2. Mix the ingredients for the pizza sauce together in a small bowl. Fill each upturned portobello mushroom with sauce, then top each with three mozzarella balls and drizzle the olive oil over.
3. Add the mushrooms to the preheated air-fryer and air-fry for 8 minutes. Serve immediately.

Broccoli Cheese

Servings: 2

Ingredients:
- 250g broccoli
- Cooking spray
- 10 tbsp evaporated milk
- 300g Mexican cheese
- 4 tsp Amarillo paste
- 6 saltine crackers

Directions:
1. Heat the air fryer to 190ºC
2. Place the broccoli in the air fryer spray with cooking oil and cook for about 6 minutes
3. Place the remaining ingredients in a blender and process until smooth
4. Place in a bowl and microwave for 30 seconds
5. Pour over the broccoli and serve

Baked Potato

Servings: 1

Ingredients:
- 1 large potato
- 1 tsp oil
- ¼ tsp onion powder
- ⅛ tsp coarse salt
- 1 tbsp of butter
- 1 tbsp of cream cheese
- 1 strip of bacon, diced
- 1 tbsp olives
- 1 tbsp chives

Directions:
1. Pierce the potato in several places with a fork, rub with oil, salt and onion powder
2. Place in the air fryer and cook at 200ºC for 35-40 minutes
3. Remove from the air fryer, cut and top with the toppings

Roasted Vegetable Pasta

Servings:4 | Cooking Time:15 Minutes

Ingredients:
- 400 g / 14 oz penne pasta
- 1 courgette, sliced
- 1 red pepper, deseeded and sliced
- 100 g / 3.5 oz mushroom, sliced
- 2 tbsp olive oil
- 1 tsp Italian seasoning
- 200 g cherry tomatoes, halved
- 2 tbsp fresh basil, chopped
- ½ tsp black pepper

Directions:
1. Cook the pasta according to the packet instructions.
2. Preheat the air fryer to 190 °C / 370 °F and line the air fryer with parchment paper or grease it with olive oil.
3. In a bowl, place the courgette, pepper, and mushroom, and toss in 2 tbsp olive oil
4. Place the vegetables in the air fryer and cook for 15 minutes.
5. Once the vegetables have softened, mix with the penne pasta, chopped cherry tomatoes, and fresh basil.
6. Serve while hot with a sprinkle of black pepper in each dish.

Mini Quiche

Servings: 2

Ingredients:
- 100g raw cashews
- 3 tbsp milk
- ½ tsp hot sauce
- 1 tsp white miso paste
- 1 tsp mustard
- 300g tofu
- 100g bacon pieces
- 1 chopped red pepper
- 1 chopped onion
- 6 tbsp yeast
- ½ tsp onion powder
- ½ tsp paprika
- ½ tsp cumin
- ½ tsp chilli powder
- ½ tsp black pepper
- ⅛ tsp turmeric
- ½ tsp canola oil
- 50g curly kale

Directions:
1. Heat the oil in a pan, add the bacon pepper, onion and curly kale and cook for about 3 minutes
2. Place all the other ingredients into a blender and blend until smooth
3. Add to a bowl with the bacon, pepper, onion and curly kale and mix well
4. Fill silicone muffin cups with the mix
5. Place in the air fryer and cook at 165ºC for 15 minutes

Saganaki

Servings: 2

Ingredients:
- 200 g/7 oz. kefalotyri or manouri cheese, sliced into wedges 1 cm/½ in. thick
- 2 tablespoons plain/all-purpose flour
- olive oil, for drizzling

Directions:
1. Preheat the air-fryer to 200ºC/400ºF.
2. Dip each wedge of cheese in the flour, then tap off any excess. Drizzle olive oil onto both sides of the cheese slices
3. Add the cheese to the preheated air-fryer and air-fry for 3 minutes. Remove from the air-fryer and serve.

Veggie Bakes

Servings: 2

Ingredients:
- Any type of leftover vegetable bake you have
- 30g flour

Directions:
1. Preheat the air fryer to 180ºC
2. Mix the flour with the leftover vegetable bake
3. Shape into balls and place in the air fryer
4. Cook for 10 minutes

Tofu Bowls

Servings: 4

Ingredients:
- 1 block of tofu, cut into cubes
- 40ml soy sauce
- 2 tbsp sesame oil
- 1 tsp garlic powder
- 1 chopped onion
- 2 tbsp Tahini dressing
- 3 bunches baby bok choy, chopped
- 300g quinoa
- 1 medium cucumber, sliced
- 1 cup shredded carrot
- 1 avocado, sliced

Directions:
1. Mix the soy sauce, 1 tbsp sesame oil and garlic powder in a bowl. Add the tofu marinade for 10 minutes
2. Place in the air fryer and cook at 200ºC for 20 minutes turning halfway
3. Heat the remaining sesame oil in a pan and cook the onions for about 4 minutes
4. Add the bok choy and cook for another 4 minutes
5. Divide the quinoa between your bowls add bok choy, carrot, cucumber and avocado. Top with the tofu and drizzle with Tahini

Rainbow Vegetables

Servings: 4

Ingredients:
- 1 red pepper, cut into slices
- 1 squash sliced
- 1 courgette sliced
- 1 tbsp olive oil
- 150g sliced mushrooms
- 1 onion sliced
- Salt and pepper to taste

Directions:
1. Preheat air fryer to 180ºC
2. Place all ingredients in a bowl and mix well
3. Place in the air fryer and cook for about 20 minutes turning halfway

Air Fryer Cheese Sandwich

Servings:2 | Cooking Time:10 Minutes

Ingredients:
- 4 slices white or wholemeal bread
- 2 tbsp butter
- 50 g / 3.5 oz cheddar cheese, grated

Directions:
1. Preheat the air fryer to 180 °C / 350 °F and line the bottom of the basket with parchment paper.
2. Lay the slices of bread out on a clean surface and butter one side of each. Evenly sprinkle the cheese on two of the slices and cover with the final two slices.
3. Transfer the sandwiches to the air fryer, close the lid, and cook for 5 minutes until the bread is crispy and golden, and the cheese is melted.

Parmesan Truffle Oil Fries

Servings: 2

Ingredients:
- 3 large potatoes, peeled and cut
- 2 tbsp truffle oil
- 2 tbsp grated parmesan
- 1 tsp paprika
- 1 tbsp parsley
- Salt and pepper to taste

Directions:
1. Coat the potatoes with truffle oil and sprinkle with seasonings
2. Add the fries to the air fryer
3. Cook at 180°C for about 15 minutes shake halfway through
4. Sprinkle with parmesan and parsley to serve

Veggie Lasagne

Servings: 1

Ingredients:
- 2 lasagne sheets
- Pinch of salt
- 100g pasta sauce
- 50g ricotta
- 60g chopped basil
- 40g chopped spinach
- 3 tbsp grated courgette

Directions:
1. Break the lasagne sheets in half, bring a pan of water to boil
2. Cook the lasagne sheets for about 8 minutes, drain and pat dry
3. Add 2 tbsp of pasta sauce to a mini loaf tin
4. Add a lasagne sheet, top with ricotta, basil and spinach, then add courgette
5. Place another lasagne sheet on top
6. Add a couple of tbsp pasta sauce, basil, spinach and courgette
7. Add the last lasagne sheet, top with pasta sauce and ricotta
8. Cover with foil and place in the air fryer
9. Cook at 180°C for 10 mins, remove foil and cook for another 3 minutes

Spring Ratatouille

Servings:2 | Cooking Time:15 Minutes

Ingredients:
- 1 tbsp olive oil
- 4 Roma tomatoes, sliced
- 2 cloves garlic, minced
- 1 courgette, cut into chunks
- 1 red pepper and 1 yellow pepper, cut into chunks
- 2 tbsp mixed herbs
- 1 tbsp vinegar

Directions:
1. Preheat the air fryer to 190 °C / 370 °F and line the air fryer with parchment paper or grease it with olive oil.
2. Place all of the ingredients into a large mixing bowl and mix until fully combined.
3. Transfer the vegetables into the lined air fryer basket, close the lid, and cook for 15 minutes until the vegetables have softened.

Roasted Garlic

Servings: 2

Ingredients:
- 1 head of garlic
- Drizzle of olive oil
- Salt and pepper for seasoning

Directions:
1. Remove paper peel from garlic
2. Place in foil and drizzle with oil
3. Place in the air fryer and cook at 200ºC for 20 minutes
4. Season before serving

Stuffed Peppers

Servings: 6

Ingredients:
- 250g diced potatoes
- 100g peas
- 1 small onion, diced
- 1 carrot, diced
- 1 bread roll, diced
- 2 garlic cloves, minced
- 2 tsp mixed herbs
- 6 bell peppers
- 100g grated cheese

Directions:
1. Preheat air fryer to 180ºC
2. Combine all the ingredients together apart from the peppers
3. Stuff the peppers with the mix
4. Place in the air fryer and cook for about 20 minutes

CHAPTER 8 SIDE DISHES RECIPES

Asparagus Spears

Servings: 2

Ingredients:
- 1 bunch of trimmed asparagus
- 1 teaspoon olive oil
- ¼ teaspoon salt
- ⅛ teaspoon freshly ground black pepper

Directions:
1. Preheat the air-fryer to 180ºC/350ºF.
2. Toss the asparagus spears in the oil and seasoning. Add these to the preheated air-fryer and air-fry for 8–12 minutes, turning once (cooking time depends on the thickness of the stalks, which should retain some bite).

Honey Roasted Parsnips

Servings: 4

Ingredients:
- 350 g/12 oz. parsnips
- 1 tablespoon plain/all-purpose flour (gluten-free if you wish)
- 1½ tablespoons runny honey
- 2 tablespoons olive oil
- salt

Directions:
1. Top and tail the parsnips, then slice lengthways, about 2 cm/¾ in. wide. Place in a saucepan with water to cover and a good pinch of salt. Bring to the boil, then boil for 5 minutes.
2. Remove and drain well, allowing any excess water to evaporate. Dust the parsnips with flour. Mix together the honey and oil in a small bowl, then toss in the parsnips to coat well in the honey and oil.
3. Preheat the air-fryer to 180ºC/350ºF.
4. Add the parsnips to the preheated air-fryer and air-fry for 14–16 minutes, depending on how dark you like the outsides (the longer you cook them, the sweeter they get).

Butternut Squash Fries

Servings: 4

Ingredients:
- 400g butternut squash, cut into sticks
- 1 tbsp olive oil
- 2 tbsp bagel seasoning
- 1 tsp fresh chopped rosemary

Directions:
1. Preheat air fryer to 200ºC
2. Drizzle butternut squash with olive oil mix to coat
3. Add to the air fryer, cook for about 22 minutes until golden brown, stirring every 4 minutes
4. Sprinkle with bagel seasoning to serve

Celery Root Fries

Servings: 2

Ingredients:
- ½ celeriac, cut into sticks
- 500ml water
- 1 tbsp lime juice
- 1 tbsp olive oil
- 75g mayo
- 1 tbsp mustard
- 1 tbsp powdered horseradish

Directions:
1. Put celeriac in a bowl, add water and lime juice, soak for 30 minutes
2. Preheat air fryer to 200
3. Mix together the mayo, horseradish powder and mustard, refrigerate
4. Drain the celeriac, drizzle with oil and season with salt and pepper
5. Place in the air fryer and cook for about 10 minutes turning halfway
6. Serve with the mayo mix as a dip

Mediterranean Vegetables

Servings: 1–2

Ingredients:
- 1 courgette/zucchini, thickly sliced
- 1 (bell) pepper, deseeded and chopped into large chunks
- 1 red onion, sliced into wedges
- 12 cherry tomatoes
- 1 tablespoon olive oil
- ½ teaspoon salt
- ½ teaspoon freshly ground black pepper
- 2 rosemary twigs
- mozzarella, fresh pesto (see page 80) and basil leaves, to serve

Directions:
1. Preheat the air-fryer to 180ºC/350ºF.
2. Toss the prepared vegetables in the oil and seasoning. Add the vegetables and the rosemary to the preheated air-fryer and air-fry for 12–14 minutes, depending on how 'chargrilled' you like them.
3. Remove and serve topped with fresh mozzarella and pesto and scattered with basil leaves.

Hasselback New Potatoes

Servings: 4

Ingredients:
- 8–12 new potatoes, roughly 5–7 cm/2–2¾ in. in length
- 2 teaspoons olive oil
- salt
- 1 tablespoon butter (optional)

Directions:
1. Preheat the air-fryer to 180ºC/350ºF.
2. Slice the potatoes multiple times widthways, making sure you do not cut all the way through (if you place the potatoes in the bowl of a wooden spoon to make these slices, it prevents you cutting all the way through). Coat the potatoes in the olive oil and sprinkle over the salt.
3. Add the potatoes to the preheated air-fryer and air-fry for 20–25 minutes until the potatoes are crispy on the outside but soft on the inside. Serve immediately.

Courgette Chips

Servings: 4

Ingredients:
- 250g panko bread crumbs
- 100g grated parmesan
- 1 medium courgette, thinly sliced
- 1 egg beaten

Directions:
1. Preheat the air fryer to 175ºC
2. Combine the breadcrumbs and parmesan
3. Dip the courgette into the egg then coat in bread crumbs
4. Spray with cooking spray and cook in the air fryer for 10 minutes
5. Turnover with tongs and cook for a further 2 minutes

Air Fryer Eggy Bread

Servings:2 | Cooking Time:5-7 Minutes

Ingredients:
- 4 slices white bread
- 4 eggs, beaten
- 1 tsp black pepper
- 1 tsp dried chives

Directions:
1. Preheat your air fryer to 150 °C / 300 °F and line the bottom of the basket with parchment paper.
2. Whisk the eggs in a large mixing bowl and soak each slice of bread until fully coated.
3. Transfer the eggy bread to the preheated air fryer and cook for 5-7 minutes until the eggs are set and the bread is crispy.
4. Serve hot with a sprinkle of black pepper and chives on top.

Potato Wedges With Rosemary

Servings: 2

Ingredients:
- 2 potatoes, sliced into wedges
- 1 tbsp olive oil
- 2 tsp seasoned salt
- 2 tbsp chopped rosemary

Directions:
1. Preheat air fryer to 190ºC
2. Drizzle potatoes with oil, mix in salt and rosemary
3. Place in the air fryer and cook for 20 minutes turning halfway

Sweet And Sticky Parsnips And Carrots

Servings:2 | Cooking Time:15 Minutes

Ingredients:
- 4 large carrots, peeled and chopped into long chunks
- 4 large parsnips, peeled and chopped into long chunks
- 1 tbsp olive oil
- 2 tbsp honey
- 1 tsp dried mixed herbs

Directions:
1. Preheat the air fryer to 150 °C / 300 °F and line the bottom of the basket with parchment paper.
2. Place the chopped carrots and parsnips in a large bowl and drizzle over the olive oil and honey. Sprinkle in some black pepper to taste and toss well to fully coat the vegetables.
3. Transfer the coated vegetables into the air fryer basket and shut the lid. Cook for 20 minutes until the carrots and parsnips and cooked and crispy.
4. Serve as a side with your dinner.

Orange Sesame Cauliflower

Servings: 4

Ingredients:
- 100ml water
- 30g cornstarch
- 50g flour
- 1/2 tsp salt
- ½ tsp pepper
- 2 tbsp tomato ketchup
- 2 tbsp brown sugar
- 1 sliced onion

Directions:
1. Mix together flour, cornstarch, water, salt and pepper until smooth
2. Coat the cauliflower and chill for 30 minutes
3. Place in the air fryer and cook for 22 minutes at 170ºC
4. Meanwhile combine remaining ingredients in a saucepan, gently simmer until thickened.
5. Mix cauliflower with sauce and top with toasted sesame seeds to serve

Sweet & Spicy Baby Peppers

Servings: 2

Ingredients:
- 200 g/7 oz. piccarella (baby) peppers, deseeded and quartered lengthways
- 1 teaspoon olive oil
- ½ teaspoon chilli/chili paste
- ¼ teaspoon runny honey
- salt and freshly ground black pepper

Directions:
1. Preheat the air-fryer to 180ºC/350ºF.
2. Toss the peppers in the oil, chilli/chili paste and honey, then add salt and pepper to taste.
3. Place in the preheated air-fryer and air-fry for 6–8 minutes, depending on how 'chargrilled' you like them, turning them over halfway through.

Shishito Peppers

Servings: 2

Ingredients:
- 200g shishito peppers
- Salt and pepper to taste
- ½ tbsp avocado oil
- 75g grated cheese
- 2 limes

Directions:
1. Rinse the peppers
2. Place in a bowl and mix with oil, salt and pepper
3. Place in the air fryer and cook at 175°C for 10 minutes
4. Place on a serving plate and sprinkle with cheese

Air Fryer Corn On The Cob

Servings: 2

Ingredients:
- 2 corn on the cob
- 2 tbsp melted butter
- A pinch of salt
- 1/2 tsp dried parsley
- 2 tbsp grated parmesan

Directions:
1. Preheat the air fryer to 270°C
2. Take a bowl and combine the melted butter, salt and parsley
3. Brush the corn with the mixture
4. Add the corn inside the air fryer and cook for 14 minutes
5. Remove the corn from the fryer and roll in the grated cheese

Garlic And Parsley Potatoes

Servings: 4

Ingredients:
- 500g baby potatoes, cut into quarters
- 1 tbsp oil
- 1 tsp salt
- ½ tsp garlic powder
- ½ tsp dried parsley

Directions:
1. Preheat air fryer to 175°C
2. Combine potatoes and oil in a bowl
3. Add remaining ingredients and mix
4. Add to the air fryer and cook for about 25 minutes until golden brown, turning halfway through

Tex Mex Hash Browns

Servings: 4

Ingredients:
- 500g potatoes cut into cubes
- 1 tbsp olive oil
- 1 red pepper
- 1 onion
- 1 jalapeño pepper
- ½ tsp taco seasoning
- ½ tsp cumin
- Salt and pepper to taste

Directions:
1. Soak the potatoes in water for 20 minutes
2. Heat the air fryer to 160°C
3. Drain the potatoes and coat with olive oil
4. Add to the air fryer and cook for 18 minutes
5. Mix the remaining ingredients in a bowl, add the potatoes and mix well
6. Place the mix into the air fryer cook for 6 minutes, shake and cook for a further 5 minutes

Mexican Rice

Servings: 4

Ingredients:
- 500g long grain rice
- 3 tbsp olive oil
- 60ml water
- 1 tsp chilli powder
- 1/4 tsp cumin
- 2 tbsp tomato paste
- 1/2 tsp garlic powder
- 1tsp red pepper flakes
- 1 chopped onion
- 500ml chicken stock
- Half a small jalapeño pepper with seeds out, chopped
- Salt for seasoning

Directions:
1. Add the water and tomato paste and combine, placing to one side
2. Take a baking pan and add a little oil
3. Wash the rice and add to the baking pan
4. Add the chicken stock, tomato paste, jalapeños, onions, and the rest of the olive oil, and combine
5. Place aluminium foil over the top and place in your air fryer
6. Cook at 220ºC for 50 minutes
7. Keep checking the rice as it cooks, as the liquid should be absorbing

Orange Tofu

Servings: 4

Ingredients:
- 400g tofu, drained
- 1 tbsp tamari
- 1 tbsp corn starch
- ¼ tsp pepper flakes
- 1 tsp minced ginger
- 1 tsp fresh garlic
- 1 tsp orange zest
- 75ml orange juice
- 75ml water
- 2 tsp cornstarch
- 1 tbsp maple syrup

Directions:
1. Cut the tofu into cubes, place in a bowl add the tamari and mix well
2. Mix in 1 tbsp starch and allow to marinate for 30 minutes
3. Place the remaining ingredients into another bowl and mix well
4. Place the tofu in the air fryer and cook at 190ºC for about 10 minutes
5. Add tofu to a pan with sauce mix and cook until sauce thickens

Roasted Okra

Servings: 1

Ingredients:
- 300g Okra, ends trimmed and pods sliced
- 1 tsp olive oil
- ¼ tsp salt
- ⅛ tsp pepper

Directions:
1. Preheat the air fryer to 175ºC
2. Combine all ingredients in a bowl and stir gently
3. Place in the air fryer and cook for 5 minutes, shake and cook for another 5 minutes

Butternut Squash

Servings: 4

Ingredients:
- 500 g/1 lb. 2 oz. butternut squash, chopped into 2.5-cm/1-in. cubes
- 1 tablespoon olive oil or avocado oil
- 1 teaspoon smoked paprika
- 1 teaspoon dried oregano
- ½ teaspoon salt
- ¼ teaspoon freshly ground black pepper

Directions:
1. Preheat the air-fryer to 180°C/350°F.
2. In a bowl toss the butternut squash cubes in the oil and all the seasonings.
3. Add the butternut squash cubes to the preheated air-fryer and air-fry for 16–18 minutes, shaking the drawer once during cooking.

Potato Wedges

Servings: 4

Ingredients:
- 2 potatoes, cut into wedges
- 1 ½ tbsp olive oil
- ½ tsp paprika
- ⅛ tsp ground black pepper
- ½ tsp parsley flakes
- ½ tsp chilli powder
- ½ tsp sea salt

Directions:
1. Preheat the air fryer to 200°C
2. Add all ingredients to a bowl and combine well
3. Place the wedges into the air fryer and cook for 10 minutes
4. Turn and cook for a further 8 minutes until golden brown

Alternative Stuffed Potatoes

Servings: 4

Ingredients:
- 4 baking potatoes, peeled and halved
- 1 tbsp olive oil
- 150g grated cheese
- ½ onion, diced
- 2 slices bacon

Directions:
1. Preheat air fryer to 175°C
2. Brush the potatoes with oil and cook in the air fryer for 10 minutes
3. Coat again with oil and cook for a further 10 minutes
4. Cut the potatoes in half spoon the insides into a bowl and mix in the cheese
5. Place the bacon and onion in a pan and cook until browned, mix in with the potato
6. Stuff the skins with the mix and return to the air fryer, cook for about 6 minutes

Pumpkin Fries

Servings: 4

Ingredients:
- 1 small pumpkin, seeds removed and peeled, cut into half inch slices
- 2 tsp olive oil
- 1 tsp garlic powder
- 1/2 tsp paprika
- A pinch of salt

Directions:
1. Take a large bowl and add the slices of pumpkin
2. Add the oil and all the seasonings. Toss to coat well
3. Place in the air fryer
4. Cook at 280°C for 15 minutes, until the chips are tender, shaking at the halfway point

Roasted Brussels Sprouts

Servings: 3

Ingredients:
- 300 g/10½ oz. Brussels sprouts, trimmed and halved
- 1 tablespoon olive oil
- ½ teaspoon salt
- ¼ teaspoon freshly ground black pepper

Directions:
1. Preheat the air-fryer to 160ºC/325ºF.
2. Toss the Brussels sprout halves in the oil and the seasoning. Add these to the preheated air-fryer and air-fry for 15 minutes, then increase the temperature of the air-fryer to 180ºC/350ºF and cook for a further 5 minutes until the sprouts are really crispy on the outside and cooked through.

Courgette Gratin

Servings: 2

Ingredients:
- 2 courgette
- 1 tbsp chopped parsley
- 2 tbsp breadcrumbs
- 4 tbsp grated parmesan
- 1 tbsp vegetable oil
- Salt and pepper to taste

Directions:
1. Heat the air fryer to 180ºC
2. Cut each courgette in half length ways then slice
3. Mix the remaining ingredients together
4. Place the courgette in the air fryer and top with the breadcrumb mix
5. Cook for about 15 minutes until golden brown

Cheesy Broccoli

Servings:4 | Cooking Time:5 Minutes

Ingredients:
- 1 large broccoli head, broken into florets
- 4 tbsp soft cheese
- 1 tsp black pepper
- 50 g / 3.5 oz cheddar cheese, grated

Directions:
1. Preheat the air fryer to 150 °C / 300 °F and line the mesh basket with parchment paper or grease it with olive oil.
2. Wash and drain the broccoli florets and place in a bowl and stir in the soft cheese and black pepper to fully coat all of the florets.
3. Transfer the broccoli to the air fryer basket and sprinkle the cheddar cheese on top. Close the lid and cook for 5-7 minutes until the broccoli has softened and the cheese has melted.
4. Serve as a side dish to your favourite meal.

Ranch-style Potatoes

Servings: 2

Ingredients:
- 300g baby potatoes, washed
- 1 tbsp olive oil
- 3 tbsp dry ranch seasoning

Directions:
1. Preheat the air fryer to 220ºC
2. Cut the potatoes in half
3. Take a mixing bowl and combine the olive oil with the ranch seasoning
4. Add the potatoes to the bowl and toss to coat
5. Cook for 15 minutes, shaking halfway through

Carrot & Parmesan Chips

Servings: 2

Ingredients:
- 180g carrots
- 1 tbsp olive oil
- 2 tbsp grated parmesan
- 1 crushed garlic clove
- Salt and pepper for seasoning

Directions:
1. Take a mixing bowl and add the olive oil and garlic, combining well
2. Remove the tops of the carrots and cut into halves, and then another half
3. Add the carrots to the bowl and toss well
4. Add the parmesan and coat the carrots well
5. Add the carrots to the air fryer and cook for 20 minutes at 220°C, shaking halfway through

Sweet Potato Tots

Servings: 24

Ingredients:
- 2 sweet potatoes, peeled
- ½ tsp cajun seasoning
- Olive oil cooking spray
- Sea salt to taste

Directions:
1. Boil the sweet potatoes in a pan for about 15 minutes, allow to cool
2. Grate the sweet potato and mix in the cajun seasoning
3. Form into tot shaped cylinders
4. Spray the air fryer with oil, place the tots in the air fryer
5. Sprinkle with salt and cook for 8 minutes at 200°C, turn and cook for another 8 minutes

Bbq Beetroot Crisps

Servings:4 | Cooking Time:5 Minutes

Ingredients:
- 400 g / 14 oz beetroot, sliced
- 2 tbsp olive oil
- 1 tbsp BBQ seasoning
- ½ tsp black pepper

Directions:
1. Preheat the air fryer to 180 °C / 350 °F and line the bottom of the basket with parchment paper.
2. Place the beetroot slices in a large bowl. Add the olive oil, BBQ seasoning, and black pepper, and toss to coat the beetroot slices on both sides.
3. Place the beetroot slices in the air fryer and cook for 5 minutes until hot and crispy.

CHAPTER 9 DESSERTS RECIPES

Peanut Butter And Banana Bites

Servings: 12

Ingredients:
- 1 banana
- 12 wonton wrappers
- 75g peanut butter
- 1-2 tsp vegetable oil

Directions:
1. Slice the banana and place in a bowl of water with lemon juice to prevent browning
2. Place one piece of banana and a spoon of peanut butter in each wonton wrapper
3. Wet the edges of each wrapper and fold over to seal
4. Spray the air fryer with oil
5. Place in the air fryer and cook at 190°C for 6 minutes

Crispy Snack Apples

Servings: 2

Ingredients:
- 3 apples, Granny Smith work best
- 250g flour
- 3 whisked eggs
- 25g sugar
- 1 tsp ground cinnamon
- 250g cracker crumbs

Directions:
1. Preheat the air fryer to 220°C
2. Peel the apples, remove the cores and cut into wedges
3. Take three bowls - the first with the flour, the second with the egg, and then this with the cracker crumbs, sugar and cinnamon combined
4. Dip the apple wedges into the egg in order
5. Place in the air fryer and cook for 5 minutes, turning over with one minute remaining

Profiteroles

Servings: 9

Ingredients:
- 100g butter
- 200g plain flour
- 6 eggs
- 300ml water
- 2 tsp vanilla extract
- 300ml whipped cream
- 100g milk chocolate
- 2 tbsp whipped cream
- 50g butter
- 2 tsp icing sugar

Directions:
1. Preheat the air fryer to 170°C
2. Place the butter and water in a pan over a medium heat, bring to the boil, remove from the heat and stir in the flour
3. Return to the heat stirring until a dough is formed
4. Mix in the eggs and stir until mixture is smooth, make into profiterole shapes and cook in the air fryer for 10 minutes
5. For the filling whisk together 300ml whipped cream, vanilla extract and the icing sugar
6. For the topping place the butter, 2tbsp whipped cream and chocolate in a bowl and melt over a pan of hot water until mixed together
7. Pipe the filling into the roles and finish off with a chocolate topping

Lemon Pies

Servings: 6

Ingredients:
- 1 pack of pastry
- 1 egg beaten
- 200g lemon curd
- 225g powdered sugar
- ½ lemon

Directions:
1. Preheat the air fryer to 180ºC
2. Cut out 6 circles from the pastry using a cookie cutter
3. Add 1 tbsp of lemon curd to each circle, brush the edges with egg and fold over
4. Press around the edges of the dough with a fork to seal
5. Brush the pies with the egg and cook in the air fryer for 10 minutes
6. Mix the lemon juice with the powdered sugar to make the icing and drizzle on the cooked pies

Apple Chips With Yogurt Dip

Servings: 4

Ingredients:
- 1 apple
- 1 tsp cinnamon
- 2 tsp oil
- Cooking spray
- 25g greek yogurt
- 1 tbsp almond butter
- 1 tsp honey

Directions:
1. Thinly slice the apple, place in a bowl and coat with cinnamon and oil
2. Coat the air fryer with cooking spray and add the apple slices
3. Cook the slices for 12 minutes at 180ºC
4. Mix the butter, honey and yogurt together and serve with the apple slices as a dip

Chocolate Orange Muffins

Servings: 12

Ingredients:
- 100g self raising flour
- 110g caster sugar
- 50g butter
- 20g cocoa powder
- 50ml milk
- 1 tsp cocoa nibs
- 1 large orange juice and rind
- 1 tbsp honey
- 1tsp vanilla essence
- 2 eggs

Directions:
1. Add the flour, butter and sugar to a mixing bowl and rug together
2. Add the cocoa, honey, orange and vanilla mix well
3. Mix the milk and egg together then add to the flour mix, combine well
4. Rub your muffin cases with flour to stop them sticking, add 2 tbsp batter to each one
5. Cook in the air fryer for 12 minutes at 180ºC

Thai Style Bananas

Servings: 4

Ingredients:
- 4 ripe bananas
- 2 tbsp flour
- 2 tbsp rice flour
- 2 tbsp corn flour
- 2 tbsp desiccated coconut
- Pinch salt
- ½ tsp baking powder
- Sesame seeds

Directions:
1. Add all the ingredients to a bowl apart from the sesame seeds mix well
2. Line the air fryer with foil
3. Dip the banana into the batter mix then roll in the sesame seeds
4. Place in the air fryer and cook for about 15 minutes at 200ºC turning halfway

Special Oreos

Servings: 9

Ingredients:
- 100g pancake mix
- 25ml water
- Cooking spray
- 9 Oreos
- 1 tbsp icing sugar

Directions:
1. Mix pancake mix and water until well combined
2. Line the air fryer with parchment paper and spray with cooking spray
3. Preheat the air fryer to 200ºC
4. Dip each cookie in the pancake mix and place in the air fryer
5. Cook for 5 minutes, turn and cook for a further 3 minutes
6. Sprinkle with icing sugar to serve

Spiced Apples

Servings: 4

Ingredients:
- 4 apples, sliced
- 2 tbsp ghee
- 2 tbsp sugar
- 1 tsp apple pie spice

Directions:
1. Place apples in a bowl, add the ghee and sprinkle with sugar and apple pie spice
2. Place in a tin that will fit the air fryer
3. Heat the air fryer to 175ºC
4. Put the tin in the air fryer and cook for 10 minutes until tender

Chocolate-glazed Banana Slices

Servings:2 | Cooking Time:10 Minutes

Ingredients:
- 2 bananas
- 1 tbsp honey
- 1 tbsp chocolate spread, melted
- 2 tbsp milk chocolate chips

Directions:
1. Preheat the air fryer to 180 °C / 350 °F. Remove the mesh basket from the machine and line it with parchment paper.
2. Cut the two bananas into even slices and place them in the lined air fryer basket.
3. In a small bowl, mix the honey and melted chocolate spread. Use a brush to glaze the banana slices. Carefully press the milk chocolate chips into the banana slices enough so that they won't fall out when you transfer the bananas into the air fryer.
4. Carefully slide the mesh basket into the air fryer, close the lid, and cook for 10 minutes until the bananas are hot and the choc chips have melted.
5. Enjoy the banana slices on their own or with a side of ice cream.

Butter Cake

Servings: 4

Ingredients:
- Cooking spray
- 7 tbsp butter
- 25g white sugar
- 2 tbsp white sugar
- 1 egg
- 300g flour
- Pinch salt
- 6 tbsp milk

Directions:
1. Preheat air fryer to 175ºC
2. Spray a small fluted tube pan with cooking spray
3. Beat the butter and all of the sugar together in a bowl until creamy
4. Add the egg and mix until fluffy, add the salt and flour mix well. Add the milk and mix well
5. Put the mix in the pan and cook in the air fryer for 15 minutes

Chocolate Orange Fondant

Servings: 4

Ingredients:
- 2 tbsp self raising flour
- 4 tbsp caster sugar
- 115g dark chocolate
- 115g butter
- 1 medium orange rind and juice
- 2 eggs

Directions:
1. Preheat the air fryer to 180ºC and grease 4 ramekins
2. Place the chocolate and butter in a glass dish and melt over a pan of hot water, stir until the texture is creamy
3. Beat the eggs and sugar together until pale and fluffy
4. Add the orange and egg mix to the chocolate and mix
5. Stir in the flour until fully mixed together
6. Put the mix into the ramekins, place in the air fryer and cook for 12 minutes. Leave to stand for 2 minutes before serving

Fried Oreos

Servings: 8

Ingredients:
- 1 tube crescent rolls
- 8 Oreos

Directions:
1. Wrap the Oreos in the crescent roll dough, trim off any excess
2. Spray the air fryer with cooking spray
3. Place Oreos in the air fryer and cook at 175ºC for 6 minutes

Chocolate Soufflé

Servings: 2

Ingredients:
- 150g semi sweet chocolate, chopped
- ¼ cup butter
- 2 eggs, separated
- 3 tbsp sugar
- ½ tsp vanilla extract
- 2 tbsp flour
- Icing sugar
- Whipped cream to serve

Directions:
1. Butter and sugar 2 small ramekins
2. Melt the chocolate and butter together
3. In another bowl beat the egg yolks, add the sugar and vanilla beat well
4. Drizzle in the chocolate mix well, add the flour and mix well
5. Preheat the air fryer to 165ºC
6. Whisk the egg whites to soft peaks, gently fold into the chocolate mix a little at a time
7. Add the mix to ramekins and place in the air fryer. Cook for about 14 minutes
8. Dust with icing sugar, serve with whipped cream

Peach Pies

Servings: 8

Ingredients:
- 2 peaches, peeled and chopped
- 1 tbsp lemon juice
- 3 tbsp sugar
- 1 tsp vanilla extract
- ¼ tsp salt
- 1 tsp cornstarch
- 1 pack ready made pastry
- Cooking spray

Directions:
1. Mix together peaches, lemon juice, sugar and vanilla in a bowl. Stand for 15 minutes
2. Drain the peaches keeping 1 tbsp of the liquid, mix cornstarch into the peaches
3. Cut the pastry into 8 circles, fill with the peach mix
4. Brush the edges of the pastry with water and fold over to form half moons, crimp the edges to seal
5. Coat with cooking spray
6. Add to the air fryer and cook at 170ºC for 12 minutes until golden brown

Chocolate And Berry Pop Tarts

Servings:8 | Cooking Time:10 Minutes

Ingredients:
- For the filling:
- 50 g / 1.8 oz fresh raspberries
- 50 g / 1.8 oz fresh strawberries
- 100 g / 3.5 oz granulated sugar
- 1 tsp corn starch
- For the pastry:
- 1 sheet puff pastry
- For the frosting:
- 4 tbsp powdered sugar
- 2 tbsp maple syrup or honey
- Chocolate sprinkles

Directions:
1. Preheat the air fryer to 180 °C / 350 °F and line the mesh basket with parchment paper or grease it with olive oil.
2. Make the filling by combining the strawberries, raspberries, and granulated sugar in a saucepan. Place on medium heat until the mixture starts to boil. When it begins to boil, turn the temperature down to a low setting. Use a spoon to break up the berries and forms a smooth mixture.
3. Stir in the corn starch and let the mixture simmer for 1-2 minutes. Remove the saucepan from the heat and set aside to cool while you prepare the pastry.
4. Roll out the large sheet of puff pastry and cut it into 8 equal rectangles.
5. Spoon 2 tbsp of the cooled berry filling onto one side of each rectangle. Fold over the other side of each puff pastry rectangle to cover the filling. Press the sides down with a fork or using your fingers to seal the filling into the pastry.
6. Transfer the puff pastry rectangles into the lined air fryer basket. Cook for 10-12 minutes until the pastry is golden and crispy.
7. Meanwhile, make the frosting. Whisk together the powdered sugar, maple syrup or honey, and chocolate chips in a bowl until well combined.
8. Carefully spread a thin layer of frosting in the centre of each pop tart. Allow the frosting to set before serving.

Chocolate Eclairs

Servings: 9

Ingredients:
- 100g plain flour
- 50g butter
- 3 eggs
- 150ml water
- 25g butter
- 1 tsp vanilla extract
- 1 tsp icing sugar
- 150ml whipped cream
- 50g milk chocolate
- 1 tbsp whipped cream

Directions:
1. Preheat the air fryer to 180°C
2. Add 50g of butter to a pan along with the water and melt over a medium heat
3. Remove from the heat and stir in the flour. Return to the heat until mix form a single ball of dough
4. Allow to cool, once cool beat in the eggs until you have a smooth dough
5. Make into eclair shapes, cook in the air fryer at 180°C for 10 minutes and then 160°C for 8 minutes
6. Mix the vanilla, icing sugar and 150ml of whipping cream until nice and thick
7. Once cool fill each eclair with the cream mix
8. Place the chocolate, 1 tbsp whipped cream and 25g of butter in a glass bowl and melt over a pan of boiling water. Top the eclairs

Key Lime Cupcakes

Servings: 6

Ingredients:
- 250g Greek yogurt
- 200g soft cheese
- 2 eggs
- Juice and rind of 2 limes
- 1 egg yolk
- ¼ cup caster sugar
- 1 tsp vanilla essence

Directions:
1. Mix the Greek yogurt and soft cheese together until smooth
2. Add the eggs and mix, add the lime juice, rind, vanilla and caster sugar and mix well
3. Fill 6 cupcake cases with the mix and place the rest to one side
4. Place in the air fryer and cook at 160°C for 10 minutes then another 10 minutes at 180°C
5. Place the remaining mix into a piping bag, once the cupcakes have cooled pipe on the top and place in the fridge to set

Banana Maple Flapjack

Servings:9

Ingredients:

- 100 g/7 tablespoons butter (or plant-based spread if you wish)
- 75 g/5 tablespoons maple syrup
- 2 ripe bananas, mashed well with the back of a fork
- 1 teaspoon vanilla extract
- 240 g/2½ cups rolled oats/quick-cooking oats

Directions:
1. Gently heat the butter and maple syrup in a medium saucepan over a low heat until melted. Stir in the mashed banana, vanilla and oats and combine all ingredients. Pour the flapjack mixture into a 15 x 15-cm/6 x 6-in. baking pan and cover with foil.
2. Preheat the air-fryer to 200°C/400°F.
3. Add the baking pan to the preheated air-fryer and air-fry for 12 minutes, then remove the foil and cook for a further 4 minutes to brown the top. Leave to cool before cutting into 9 squares.

Apple Pie

Servings: 2

Ingredients:
- 1 packet of ready made pastry
- 1 apple, chopped
- 2 tsp lemon juice
- 1 tsp cinnamon
- 2 tbsp sugar
- ½ tsp vanilla extract
- 1 tbsp butter
- 1 beaten egg
- 1 tbsp raw sugar

Directions:
1. Preheat the air fryer to 160ºC
2. Line a baking tin with pastry
3. Mix the apple, lemon juice, cinnamon, sugar and vanilla in a bowl
4. Pour the apple mix into the tin with the pastry, top with chunks of butter
5. Cover with a second piece of pastry, place three slits in the top of the pastry
6. Brush the pastry with beaten egg and sprinkle with raw sugar
7. Place in the air fryer and cook for 30 minutes

Brazilian Pineapple

Servings: 2

Ingredients:
- 1 small pineapple, cut into spears
- 100g brown sugar
- 2 tsp cinnamon
- 3 tbsp melted butter

Directions:
1. Mix the brown sugar and cinnamon together in a small bowl
2. Brush the pineapple with melted butter
3. Sprinkle with the sugar and cinnamon
4. Heat the air fryer to 200ºC
5. Cook the pineapple for about 10 minutes

Peach Pies

Servings: 8

Ingredients:
- 2 peaches, peeled and chopped
- 1 tbsp lemon juice
- 3 tbsp sugar
- 1 tsp vanilla extract
- ¼ tsp salt
- 1 tsp cornstarch
- 1 pack of shortcrust pastry

Directions:
1. Stir together peaches, lemon juice, sugar, vanilla and salt allow to stand for 15 minutes
2. Drain the peaches keeping 1 tbsp of the juice
3. Mix the liquid with the cornstarch and mix into the peaches
4. Cut out 8 4 inch circles from the pastry. Add 1 tbsp of peach mix to each piece of pastry
5. Fold the dough over to create half moons, crimp the edges with a fork to seal. Spray with cooking spray
6. Place in the air fryer and cook at 180ºC for 12-14 minutes

Pumpkin Spiced Bread Pudding

Servings: 2

Ingredients:
- 175g heavy cream
- 500g pumpkin puree
- 30ml milk
- 25g sugar
- 1 large egg, plus one extra yolk
- ⅛ tsp salt
- ½ tsp pumpkin spice
- 500g cubed crusty bread
- 4 tbsp butter

Directions:
1. Place all of the ingredients apart from the bread and butter into a bowl and mix.
2. Add the bread and melted butter to the bowl and mix well
3. Heat the air fryer to 175ºC
4. Pour the mix into a baking tin and cook in the air fryer for 35-40 minutes
5. Serve with maple cream

Thai Fried Bananas

Servings: 8

Ingredients:
- 4 ripe bananas
- 2 tbsp flour
- 2 tbsp rice flour
- 2 tbsp cornflour
- 2 tbsp desiccated coconut
- Pinch salt
- ½ tsp baking powder
- ½ tsp cardamon powder

Directions:

1. Place all the dry ingredients in a bowl and mix well. Add a little water at a time and combine to form a batter

2. Cut the bananas in half and then half again length wise

3. Line the air fryer with parchment paper and spray with cooking spray

4. Dip each banana piece in the batter mix and place in the air fryer

5. Cook at 200ºC for 10 -15 minutes turning halfway

6. Serve with ice cream

Baked Nectarines

Servings: 4

Ingredients:
- 2 teaspoons maple syrup
- 1 teaspoon vanilla extract
- 1 teaspoon ground cinnamon
- 4 nectarines, halved and stones/pits removed
- chopped nuts, yogurt and runny honey, to serve (optional)

Directions:

1. Preheat the air-fryer to 180ºC/350º F.

2. Mix the maple syrup, vanilla extract and cinnamon in a ramekin or shake in a jar to combine. Lay the nectarine halves on an air-fryer liner or piece of pierced parchment paper. Drizzle over the maple syrup mix.

3. Place in the preheated air-fryer and air-fry for 9–11 minutes, until soft when pricked with a fork. Serve scattered with chopped nuts and with a generous dollop of yogurt. Drizzle over some honey if you wish.

Zebra Cake

Servings: 6

Ingredients:
- 115g butter
- 2 eggs
- 100g caster sugar
- 1 tbsp cocoa powder
- 100g self raising flour
- 30ml milk
- 1tsp vanilla

Directions:

1. Preheat air fryer to 160ºC

2. Line a 6 inch baking tin

3. Beat together the butter and sugar until light and fluffy

4. Add eggs one at a time then add the vanilla and milk

5. Add the flour and mix well

6. Divide the mix in half

7. Add cocoa powder to half the mix and mix well

8. Add a scoop of each of the batters at a time until it's all in the tin, place in the air fryer and cook for 30 minutes

Grain-free Millionaire's Shortbread

Servings:9 | **Ingredients:**

- BASE
- 60 g/5 tablespoons coconut oil
- 1 tablespoon maple syrup
- ½ teaspoon vanilla extract
- 180 g/1¾ cups ground almonds
- a pinch of salt
- MIDDLE
- 185 g/1⅓ cups dried pitted dates (soak in hot water for at least 20 minutes, then drain)
- 2 tablespoons almond butter
- 90 g/scant ½ cup canned coconut milk (the thick part once it has separated is ideal)
- TOPPING
- 125 g/½ cup coconut oil
- 4 tablespoons cacao powder
- 1 tablespoon maple syrup

Directions:

1. Preheat the air-fryer to 180ºC/350ºF.
2. To make the base, in a small saucepan melt the coconut oil with the maple syrup and vanilla extract. As soon as the coconut oil is melted, stir in the almonds and the salt off the heat. Press this mixture into a 15 x 15-cm/6 x 6-in. baking pan.
3. Add the baking pan to the preheated air-fryer and cook for 4 minutes, until golden brown on top. Remove from the air-fryer and allow to cool.
4. In a food processor, combine the rehydrated drained dates, almond butter and coconut milk. Once the base is cool, pour this mixture over the base and pop into the freezer to set for an hour.
5. After the base has had 45 minutes in the freezer, make the topping by heating the coconut oil in a saucepan until melted, then whisk in the cacao powder and maple syrup off the heat to make a chocolate syrup. Leave this to cool for 15 minutes, then pour over the set middle layer and return to the freezer for 30 minutes. Cut into 9 squares to serve.

Lemon Tarts

Servings: 8

Ingredients:

- 100g butter
- 225g plain flour
- 30g caster sugar
- Zest and juice of 1 lemon
- 4 tsp lemon curd

Directions:

1. In a bowl mix together butter, flour and sugar until it forms crumbs, add the lemon zest and juice
2. Add a little water at a time and mix to form a dough
3. Roll out the dough and line 8 small ramekins with it
4. Add ¼ tsp of lemon curd to each ramekin
5. Cook in the air fryer for 15 minutes at 180ºC

Banana And Nutella Sandwich

Servings: 2

Ingredients:

- Softened butter
- 4 slices white bread
- 25g chocolate spread
- 1 banana

Directions:

1. Preheat the air fryer to 185ºC
2. Spread butter on one side of all the bread slices
3. Spread chocolate spread on the other side of each slice
4. Add sliced banana to two slices of bread then add the other slice of bread to each
5. Cut in half diagonally to form triangles
6. Place in the air fryer and cook for 5 minutes turn over and cook for another 2 minutes

Strawberry Lemonade Pop Tarts

Servings: 12

Ingredients:

- 300g whole wheat flour
- 225g white flour
- ¼ tsp salt
- 2 tbsp light brown sugar
- 300g icing sugar
- 2 tbsp lemon juice
- Zest of 1 lemon
- 150g cold coconut oil
- 1 tsp vanilla extract
- 75ml ice cold water
- Strawberry Jam
- 1 tsp melted coconut oil
- ¼ tsp vanilla extract
- Sprinkles

Directions:

1. In a bowl mix the flours, salt and sugar. Mix in the cold coconut oil
2. Add 1 tsp vanilla and 1 tbsp at a time of the ice cold water, mix until a dough is formed
3. Take the dough and roll out thinly on a floured surface. Cut into 5cm by 7cm rectangles
4. Place a tsp of jam in the centre of half the rectangles, wet the edges place another rectangle on the top and seal
5. Place in the air fryer and cook at 200ºC for 10 minutes. Allow to cool
6. Mix the icing sugar, coconut oil, lemon juice and lemon zest in a bowl. Mix well. Top the pop tarts and add sprinkles to serve

APPENDIX : RECIPES INDEX

C

O

P

Q

R

S

Printed in Great Britain
by Amazon

17216874R00061